No Standing Around in My Gym

5 Pride

No Standing Around in My Gym

J. D. Hughes

Human Kinetics

Library of Congress Cataloging-in-Publication Data

Hughes, J. D., 1972-
  No standing around in my gym / J.D. Hughes
    p. cm.
Includes bibliographical references.
  ISBN 0-7360-4179-6
  1. Physical education for children. 2. Games. I. Title.
  GV443 .H74 2003
  372.86--dc21

                            2002008452

ISBN-10: 0-7360-4179-6
ISBN-13: 978-0-7360-4179-9

The Web addresses cited in this text were current as of August 6, 2002, unless otherwise noted.

Acquisitions Editor: Scott Wikgren; **Developmental Editor:** Patricia A. Norris, PhD; **Assistant Editor:** Lee Alexander; **Copyeditor:** Scott J. Weckerly; **Proofreader:** Kathy Bennett; **Permission Manager:** Dalene Reeder; **Graphic Designer:** Nancy Rasmus; **Graphic Artist:** Dawn Sills; **Cover Designer:** Jack W. Davis; **Cover Illustrator:** Dick Flood; **Art Manager:** Kelly Hendren; **Illustrator:** Fred Gordy; **Printer:** Versa Press

Printed in the United States of America   15   14   13   12   11

The paper in this book is certified under a sustainable forestry program.

Human Kinetics
Web site: www.HumanKinetics.com

United States: Human Kinetics, P.O. Box 5076, Champaign, IL 61825-5076
800-747-4457
email: humank@hkusa.com

Canada: Human Kinetics, 475 Devonshire Road Unit 100, Windsor, ON N8Y 2L5
800-465-7301 (in Canada only)
email: info@hkcanada.com

Europe: Human Kinetics, 107 Bradford Road, Stanningley, Leeds LS28 6 AT, United Kingdom
+44 (0) 113 255 5665
email: hk@hkeurope.com

Australia: Human Kinetics, 57A Price Avenue, Lower Mitcham, South Australia 5062
08 8372 0999
e-mail: info@hkaustralia.com

New Zealand: Human Kinetics, Division of Sports Distributors NZ Ltd., P.O. Box 300 226 Albany,
North Shore City, Auckland
0064 9 448 1207
e-mail: info@humankinetics.co.nz

I dedicate this book to my loving wife and baby girls,
Elizabeth, Janie, and Josie. Thank you for the never-ending support,
inspiration, love, and prayer. I will love and cherish you always.

To Dad and Mom—your love for children is to this day
still evident and has rubbed off on me. Thank you for the life
you provided me with and for your unconditional love.

With my deepest love,
J.D. Hughes

Contents

Part I   Physical Education Units, Games, and Activities That Involve Everyone

Part II   Supplemental Ideas for Physical Education

Game Finder

P = preschool; K = kindergarten; 1 = first grade; 2 = second grade; 3 = third grade; 4 = fourth grade; 5 = fifth grade.

Preface

I offer a resource that cannot be connected to the old-school, roll-the-ball-out kinds of thinking that are associated with physical education's past. I longed to create a book that would assist educators in developing, improving, and facilitating instructional practices in such a way that it would produce a desirable shift toward quality physical education.

I have had numerous opportunities to research activities and lessons for my physical education program, especially while completing my masters of education and educational specialists program. During this time, I obtained valuable information, especially during my research project. In my research thesis, I developed an attitude scale to assess students' perceptions about physical education, and I came across some shocking facts that simply supported my desire for writing a book of this nature.

DeMarco and Sidney (1990) put it best when they reported that a problem lies in the fact that in many elementary physical education classes, students are offered inappropriate activities with insufficient intensity to develop cardiorespiratory fitness. Graham et al. (1992) made another interesting point when they encouraged teachers to question the fitness activities used in physical education. For example, does it matter if students list fitness activities as not being fun? Can teachers design activities to achieve fitness goals that children also find enjoyable? Are teachers responsible for students associating fitness with unpleasantness and for turning students away from becoming physically fit?

This point is significant because teachers, parents, and physical educators rate the development of a good attitude toward participation in physical activity as one of the most important objectives of a physical education program (Schutz et al. 1985). In fact, Tinning and Fitzclarance (1992) suggested another alarming point that up to 20% of children (elementary or school-age) do not even enjoy participating in physical education. In addition, there are indicators that a growing percentage of youth find physical activity less relevant and less enjoyable than youth did in previous years. According to the U.S. Department of Health and Human Services (1996), more than 60% of Americans are not regularly active and nearly half of youths (12-21) are not vigorously active on a regular basis.

We can jump to the logical assumption that fewer children are active. Educators cannot (and should not) take lightly the current attitudes toward physical education. In response to this growing apathy, we need to ask ourselves the following questions: One, are we responsible for the students' attitudes toward physical education and fitness? (I think so!) Second, do we want to be responsible for reinforcing some of the negative attitudes attributed to physical education by parents and students? (I think not!)

Our task is a challenging one. Physical educators work hard and full days that leave very little time for creative thinking and lesson plan exploration. Often times, teachers implement lessons and games that are fun to teach, but they may be activities that fail to maximize participation, that are developmentally inappropriate, or lack originality. Another problem is that some physical educators find their classes too large to even consider many physical education ideas and activities. And in many cases, physical education programs simply lack creative and innovative unit plans, parent support and involvement, or up-to-date classroom and behavior management ideas. No question—these are just a few of the major problems facing many physical educators every day.

No Standing Around in My Gym, however, will be a breath of fresh air to those who feel the above statements are true. This book saves valuable preparation time by allowing physical educators to select from an array of proven, well-balanced games and units. This resource is a guide for enhancing any program's educational potential for elementary and middle school physical educators, recreation directors, and gymnasium facilitators alike. This stimulating assortment of fun-packed, educational units, games, and ideas not only focuses on participation and involvement for the large class, but it will intrigue, engage, and motivate your students for years to come. This resource provides invigorating activities, which in turn minimize discipline problems and maximize participation.

This book provides educators with an up-to-date look at how physical education has evolved into an exciting and dynamic experience that every child needs and deserves. Over my seven-year experience as a physical education specialist, I have developed, designed, modified, or obtained from colleagues all of the material presented in this book, and I have divided it all into two main parts. Part I presents physical education units, games, and activities that involve everyone. Chapter 1 provides six units of instruction while chapter 2 introduces a variety of supporting games and activities for teachers to choose from. Part II offers supplemental ideas for physical education. The three chapters in this part provide ideas for behavior and class management, student incentives and motivational ideas, as well as how to inform and educate the parents.

The units, games, and activities described in part I are classroom-tested and have been used successfully with children ages 4 to 11. They maximize participation and ensure that every child is provided with numerous opportunities for success while learning basic fitness- and sport-related skills. With these activities, I have focused special emphasis on experiences that teach cooperation by encouraging teamwork and that improve self-esteem, initiative, and creative thinking by facilitating dynamic social interaction. These values are instilled through motivating and challenging activities that will have all children coming back for more.

Although I haven't focused attention on the how-tos of individual and team sports, readers will find that the major essential skills and objectives of most sports and physical education are taught in what's called *station format*. This proven teaching methodology provides an environment conducive for skill acquisition and learning. It requires less equipment while maximizing class participation by grouping students into small units that rotate from six to eight skill stations.

Implementing the station format approach also enables teachers to monitor student performance while assisting those students who demonstrate performances inconsistent with the learning goals. Being able to monitor the various ongoing stations, instead of teaching one skill and observing the whole class, is not only convenient, but it helps eliminate most of the behavior problems. For example, a teacher can observe the children as they rotate through basketball stations. They can then focus on any one student's shooting technique to determine if it is successful, accidental, or consistently poor. If necessary, the teacher can step in, not too prematurely, and offer the necessary suggestions or feedback to correct any problem.

This methodology works well because the station format allows the students to create their own challenges. The challenges are endless, and what is ideal is that the challenges are self-imposed. In addition, students rarely get bored because they know that they will be rotating to a new station every four to six minutes.

The station format system can also be used as an alternative to the skills and fitness tests associated with elementary physical education. Teachers can create a more positive environment with the station format because of its ease of implementation, its greater number of simultaneous skills and participation, and its improvement of the students' self-esteem and interest. Failure simply does not exist because an educator can provide optimal opportunities for success and achievement for each student, at the same time.

In a nonthreatening environment, where the focus is solely on numerous opportunities for improvement (not just performance), each student develops confidence in skills acquisition of any nature. High degrees of competence lead to confidence, which encourages children to try, enjoy, and participate in a lifetime of physical activities and sports. These coeducational units and games provide flexibility in that educators can easily (1) supplement them with other units and games in this book, (2) combine them with any already established units, and (3) modify them in any way to best meet curricular needs. The lessons and games contain easy-to-read illustrations and diagrams to aid in class setup and equipment placement. Although most lessons and games are set up to use standard physical education equipment, additional equipment may be appropriate.

Although disciplining students can be one of the least favorite jobs of teaching, employing proven techniques to reduce inappropriate behavior is a necessary task. I address this aspect in both parts of the book with ideas to help you implement enjoyable, success-oriented experiences that discourage negative behavior. Part I includes gym-tested strategies for behavior and classroom management. Implementing these strategies (whole or part) in combination with any already established methods produces appropriate behavior and thus ensures a quality learning experience. Part II provides the program facilitator with student incentives and motivational ideas that positively affect (although perhaps indirectly) each student's level of physical activity, involvement, performance, and morale. This in turn significantly influences desirable shifts in student behavior and participation.

As a result of a well-designed physical education program, the overall goal is that children develop healthy attitudes that eventually lead them to a lifestyle of regular physical activity. To dismiss any negative parental attitudes, educators need to communicate to parents the important contribution physical education makes toward the quality of each child's entire life. Part II contains examples of ways to educate parents on what their children learn and do in physical education and to inform them of upcoming events. From physical education brochures to informative newsletters, it is important to help parents, teachers, administrators, and the communities involved realize how important and necessary a quality physical education program is to overall wellness, which is really the ultimate aim of this book.

As physical education teachers, it is our job to shift the current attitude of students toward physical activity. We not only want them to understand its value, but we also really want them to simply learn to *enjoy* it. So let *No Standing Around in My Gym* help guide you toward greater success in your physical education program and the important goal of seeing students have some fun in the gym. Best of luck.

Acknowledgments

First and foremost, I would like to thank my Lord and Savior, Jesus Christ who allows me to be a part of this wonderful profession each day and who continually shows me that His grace is sufficient.

This book represents a noble group of colleagues and friends who, every day, contribute their lives to serving students and who through their examples and ideas were instrumental in the creation of this book:

Dr. Lynne Gaskin

Tara Arbegast

Raymond "Butch" Soles

April Barton

Teresa Paini

Bright Star Elementary School

Physical education specialists everywhere

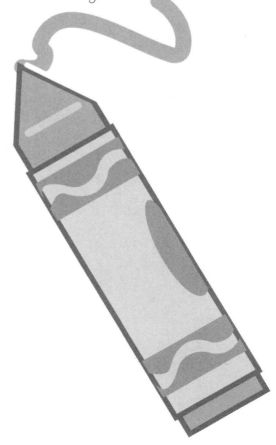

Part I

Physical Education Units, Games, and Activities That Involve Everyone

In part I, I present six physical education units and many activities and games to help teachers plan classes for kindergarten through fifth grade. The station format offers opportunities for teachers to observe and supervise many children participating in a variety of activities at the same time. The wide choice of games and activities presented provides motivation for the children and sustains their interest over the entire semester.

Chapter 1
Physical Education Units

This chapter contains exciting unit ideas designed to provide participation activities for physical education classes involving 50 to 75 elementary children at a time. Please note that unit ideas on a particular sport or activity are not exhaustive or in any particular order. They are simply ideas set up in one- to two-week units. Placing activities into one- to two-week units is a proven way to eliminate the onset of boredom or burnout. It is a method based on the premise that children need a variety of skills, activities, and challenges to keep them motivated and attentive. As you read this chapter, consider these tips to help maximize your lessons and meet your program's needs.

■ You will find that the skills of most sports are provided in station format, a proven technique that provides skills acquisition, requires less equipment, and maximizes class participation and socialization (see the Six Station layout and the two Eight Station layouts for examples of gym setup on pages 4-5). When you implement the station format, always have the equipment placed in its appropriate area before classes arrive. Demonstrate the activity and its rules at each station. Use two signals to prepare students to rotate—music and a whistle work well. The first signal reminds students to put all equipment in its appropriate place; the second signal allows them to move to the next station *only* after all groups have prepared their station for the next group. Choose a consistent direction for students to rotate, either clockwise or counterclockwise, and remember to reinforce that direction.

■ Note the grade-level appropriateness located at the beginning of the unit. *P* stands for pre-kindergarten; other classes are designated kindergarten through fifth grade.

■ You can modify any of the P-2 units for third, fourth, and fifth grades by varying equipment or spatial needs.

■ Consider the time of year, season, and weather conditions when determining lesson plan compatibility, especially when the gym is not the ideal place for the activity.

■ Modify equipment, spatial, or station needs for classes of 30 or fewer students.

■ Try the following partnering and grouping methods. These ideas place the responsibility of choosing groups on the students and off the teacher. In case problems arise within a group, remind students that they choose their groups and are responsible for following class rules and working together.

❑ Perform a 10-second countdown at the beginning of class to quickly group students or to instruct them to find a personal space on the floor. For example, the teacher says "groups of four" and begins the 10-second countdown. During the countdown, students choose their own groups, then immediately see the teacher, who instructs them to go to a particular area or to start at a certain station.

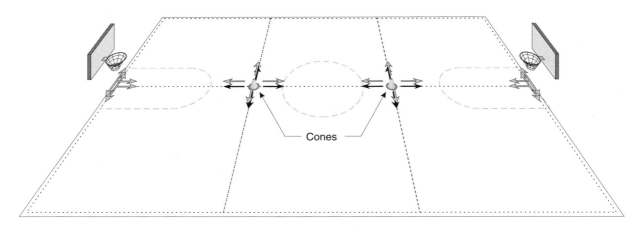

Six Station Layout

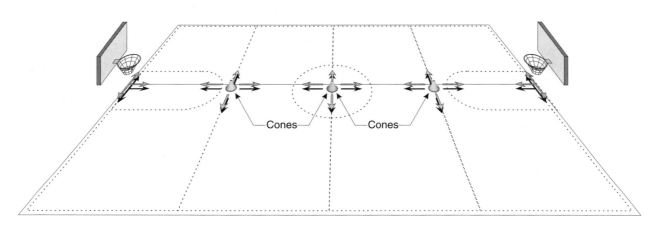

Eight Station Layout *(a)*

❑ Use a whistle blow. Students learn to react to this great nonverbal cue. Students get into groups based on how many times the whistle blows. For example, the teacher quickly gives six short and loud whistle blows, briefly followed by another six short and loud whistle blows. (The signal is given twice in case students were not listening the first time.) Students react quickly by choosing their groups of six, who then see the teacher for instructions to go to a particular area or to start at a certain station.

❑ For grouping a class, instruct students once they arrive to go to any group, put on a color jersey, and wait for further instructions. When playing Outbreak, for example, the teacher places the jerseys for six groups into their designated spots before classes arrive. If no jerseys are available for one group, then students must go to another area until all the jerseys are taken. The teacher then adds any additional jerseys only after all the jerseys are taken. This is a great idea for many of the games in this book.

■ For additional resources, see the "Suggested Readings and References" section in the back of the book.

■ At the end of many units, I have included "Games and Activities" sections that detail fun and exciting games to help reinforce previously learned skills.

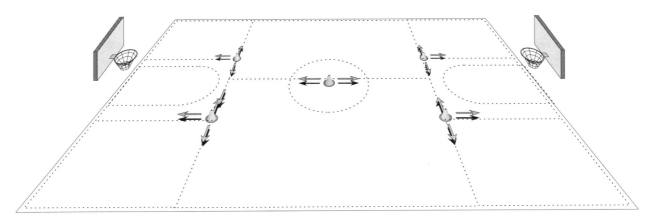

Eight Station Layout (b)

◼ Because many units are set up in station format, they can be either combined with other units and games or modified in any way that best meets your school's curricular needs.

◼ This resource does not include skills tests or formal and informal assessments. To ensure that program objectives and guidelines are covered and met, however, you can create assessments by utilizing the skills and concepts presented in this book.

Please remember that the systems for equipment setup and dispersion, the signals for starting and stopping class, and the methods for dealing with behavior problems are necessary time management components that help facilitate and ensure overall success for each unit you teach. See "Ideas for Behavior and Class Management" in chapter 3 for examples.

Ball Handling and Manipulative Skills

The following lead-up activities should be introduced before implementing any supporting games or formal sports. The overall goal is to develop high degrees of coordination and competence, which in turn, will lead to confidence that encourages children to try, enjoy, and participate in a variety of physical activities and lifelong sports.

Ball Challenges (3-5)

Objective

To develop, refine, and enhance hand-eye coordination and strategy through a variety of exciting and challenging ball activities.

Equipment

- ◼ Hula hoops (15)
- ◼ Beanbags, Z-Balls™, Hacky Sacks®, bungee balls, tennis balls, and playground balls (5 each)
- ◼ Five-gallon buckets and Gatorskin™ balls (10 each)
- ◼ Poly spots or floor tape
- ◼ Basketballs, yarn balls, rubber chickens, or any sort of object suitable for throwing can be used for Partner Juggle or Mind Freeze (optional)
- ◼ Traffic cones (to section off each station)

Procedure

Demonstrate each activity station (rules and how to play). Divide students into equal groups and assign them to one of the six stations presented in this section. Each group rotates to a new station every four to six minutes. Choose from the following list the stations that work best for you—eliminate or add stations to adjust for class size or available equipment.

Note: If enough equipment is available, large classes can play many of these games separately.

Games and Activities

- Bowling Bombs
- In the Zone
- Cross Over Craze
- Pin Bombardment
- Dr. Feelgood
- Team Trashball
- Gator Bait
- Toxic Blast

Hoop It

This is a great game to introduce both offensive and defensive positions and strategies. Students partner up; each getting into a hula hoop approximately 10 to 15 feet apart. Use floor tape or some type of floor marking to show where hoops should be in case they get moved. To begin, players with a beanbag (standing in their hoops) try to toss the beanbag so that it lands and remains inside their opponents' hoop. (The rule of the beanbag staying inside the hoop to get a point was established to deter players from throwing too hard.) The defenders attempt to block the beanbags in any way to keep it from landing inside their hoops. The offensive players get one point when their beanbag stays inside the hoop. Score or no score, the defenders now are on offense, attempting to score against their opponents. Play until someone scores 3, 5, or 10 points. There are lots of methods you can try. You decide.

Z-Ball Challenge

This wacky game will have them tossin' and turnin'. Students partner up and get one Z-Ball. To begin, the player with the Z-Ball drops the ball from waist level toward the opponent (no throwing). The opponents must decide on which bounce to catch it because they get one point for each bounce the Z-Ball makes before it is caught. For example, if a player catches it on the third bounce, that catch is worth three points. Any contact with the ball that does not result in a catch is awarded no points. Take turns after every serve. Note: Don't let this game fool you because Z-Balls are known for their wacky bounces. You never know where it is going to bounce after the first bounce. Play until someone scores 3, 5, or 10 points. There are lots of methods you can try.

Mind Freeze

Each group of five or more gets one Gatorskin ball, then forms a circle. To begin, the group starts a tossing pattern by tossing the ball to the same person each time, preferably someone who is across from them. All groups must follow whatever tossing pattern they develop. When the established tossing pattern is mastered with one ball, simply add a different ball or unique object to make it more challenging. Remember to toss it to the same person. Create new tossing and bouncing patterns to challenge each group. *Guess what, ya'll are now group juggling!*

Bucket Bash

Students partner up and get one tennis ball and two five-gallon buckets. All players stand across from their partner (approximately 10 to 15 feet apart) with their buckets placed in front of them. Use floor tape or some type of floor marking to show where buckets should always be in case they get moved. To begin, one player starts the game by bouncing the tennis ball one time, attempting to aim and score it in the opposing member's bucket. A player receives one point each time a tennis ball lands and stays in the bucket. Take turns after every serve. Note: Each player must stand behind the bucket, and each player must catch the ball if it misses the bucket after the second bounce. Play until someone scores 3, 5, or 10 points. Again, there are lots of methods you can try.

10' to 15'

Partner Juggle

Students partner up, get two Gatorskin balls, then stand on poly spots or markers placed on the floor approximately five feet apart. To begin, each pair tosses their balls back and forth at the same time, attempting to catch them. The teacher then gives verbal challenges: (1) How many catches can you make before one of you drops a ball? (2) How fast can you go before a ball is dropped? (3) Can one partner toss the ball while the other person bounces it? (4) Can you make up your own partner juggle? (5) If there is an odd number, try three-person juggling in a triangle, then try the challenges just mentioned. *Watch it! This one gets you dizzy.*

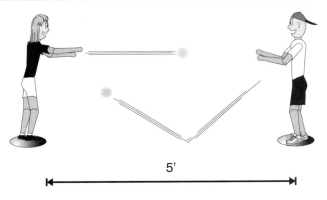

5'

Hoop Rally

Adapted from the game Four-Square, Hoop Rally is an invigorating, fast-paced game of speed and agility. Students partner up and get one hula hoop and playground ball. To begin, place the hula hoop on the floor. The player with the ball drops and bats the ball inside the hoop to the opposing player. The opposing player must return the serve by batting the ball back into the hoop. Remind students that the batted ball must bounce one time inside the hoop before being returned. The object of Hoop Rally is to bat the ball in a way that it cannot be returned, which is worth

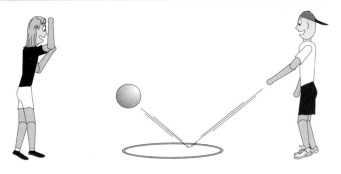

one point. Points are also scored if the ball bounces more than once or if the ball is caught. The scoring player starts the ball for the next volley. Play until someone scores 3, 5, or 10 points. An interesting fact is that when children play this game long enough, they start to develop new and wacky rules of their own.

Group Hacky Sack®

The object of this game is to see how many times the group can contact the Hacky Sack before it hits the ground. Until students get the knack of it, allow them to use their hands.

Bungee Ball

Bungee balls, sometimes known as Yo-Yo Balls™, improve hand-eye coordination and tracking skills. Bungee balls consist of a wrist strap with a bungee and ball attached to it. Instruct students to simply throw the ball away from their body and try to catch it when it comes back to them.

Ball Manipulation (P-2)

Objective

To develop, enhance, and improve ball manipulation skills such as visual tracking, accuracy, control, throwing, catching, right- and left-handed manipulation, and socialization skills through the use of playground balls.

Equipment

Playground or Nerf™ ball (1 per student)

Procedure

To start class, direct the children that to receive a playground ball, each must sit down in a personal space and get quiet before the 10-second countdown is up. Choose from the following activities the ideas that will work best for you. This list is not exhaustive. Feel free to add or eliminate ideas to meet the class objective.

Student or teacher should demonstrate the following:

- Roll the ball around body parts (seat, thighs, head, one knee, two knees)
  - ❑ while sitting or standing, and
  - ❑ along the floor around your feet (figure eight pattern on and off the floor).
- Dribble with dominant hand (use finger pads).
  - ❑ Switch hands and dribble with nondominant hand.
  - ❑ Dribble slowly or quickly—at low, medium, and high levels.
  - ❑ Dribble high-to-low or low-to-high.
  - ❑ Dribble close to yourself, then far away.
  - ❑ Dribble while kneeling on one knee, moving forward, backward, and sideways.
  - ❑ Dribble around the room using the various locomotor movements in various pathways.
  - ❑ Make up a new skill, or practice previously learned skills (and perform it to music).
- Two-handed toss—catch at low, medium, and high levels.

- ❑ Toss, turn, catch.
- ❑ Toss, clap, catch.
- ❑ Toss, turn around, bounce, catch.
- ❑ Toss, bounce, turn around, catch.
- ❑ Toss and catch while jumping, hopping, or jogging.
- ❑ Invent your own toss and catch, then show someone.

- ■ Rolling and fielding a ball back and forth (*How fast or slow can you roll it to your partner?*). Partner children up and instruct each group to V-sit (sit down with legs separated) about five yards apart. If there are an odd number of students, instruct students to form a triangle.

  - ❑ Stand and perform two-handed, underhand rolls, then turn around and roll the ball through your legs.
  - ❑ Invent a new way to roll it to your partner.

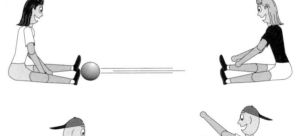

- ■ Partner passes with hands or feet. Children remain in partners. If there is an uneven number of children, create one triangle of students.

  - ❑ Chest or bounce pass.
  - ❑ "Squish the bug": Step, push from chest, arms out, and thumbs down.
  - ❑ Always catch the ball with two hands.
  - ❑ Bounce it to your partner who then rolls it back (and vice versa).
  - ❑ Try passing and trapping the ball with your feet, like in soccer.
  - ❑ What other ways can you think of to get the ball to your partner?

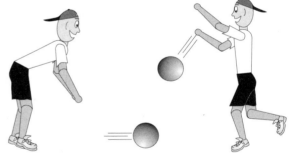

Rules and Safety

- ■ Keep your ball in your area.
- ■ Never kick the balls.

Games and Activities

- ■ Bowling Bombs
- ■ Cross Over Craze
- ■ Dr. Feelgood
- ■ Gator Bait
- ■ In the Zone
- ■ Pin Bombardment
- ■ Swamp Ball

■ Team Trashball
■ Toxic Blast

Basketball Skills (P-2)

Objective

To introduce and develop basketball dribbling, shooting, guarding, and passing skills at various basketball stations.

Equipment

■ Basketballs (20) (If available, different colored balls at each station really help students distinguish which balls go where.)

■ Basketball goals at a 7-foot or 8-foot level (6) (Wall-mounted brackets for the side goals work great! See physical education catalogs for mountable wall brackets. These brackets hold rims that can be removed after use. If enough goals are not available, use big garbage cans.)

■ Traffic cones (to section off each station)

Procedure

Demonstrate each activity station (rules and how to play), and divide students into equal groups to play at each station. Choose from the following list which stations work best for you, and eliminate or add stations to complement your class size or available equipment.

Before you send the students off to each station, take the opportunity to demonstrate how to hold a basketball. With the shooting arm bent like an *L*, use the other hand to help balance the ball, bend the legs, then shoot towards the goal.

Games and Activities

■ Dribbling: Children practice ball-handling skills on their own. Make sure to demonstrate the walking and double-dribble rules.

■ Weave Dribbling: Children form four to six lines and zigzag in and out of the poly spots while dribbling a basketball.

■ Chest or Bounce Pass: Children practice the chest and bounce pass to one another. To show them where to stand, place poly spots on the ground. Look for these things: (1) "squishing the bug," or taking a step toward the person being passed to, (2) pushing from the chest, (3) good follow-through with arms extended toward partner, hands out, and thumbs down.

Copycat

Students partner up and decide who goes first. The shooting partner from each group chooses a spot from anywhere within the boundaries to shoot. If the shooting partner misses the shot, then the nonshooting partner shoots from any different spot within the boundaries. On the other hand, if the original shooter makes the shot, then the nonshooting partner must now attempt to shoot and make it (the copycat shot) from the exact same spot. If the copycat shooter misses the shot, a second chance is always allowed. If the copycat shooter misses the second shot, one point is given to the other person. Start a new round by selecting a new shot. *How many points can you get? Can you attempt a really hard shot? Can you make a really goofy shot for your partner to attempt?*

Spot Shot

Use five to seven poly spots or bases as markers on the floor to form a semicircle around the goal. Each child partners up and decides who goes first. The object for each player is to go from the first spot on one side all the way to the last spot on the other side by making each shot. The shooter's partner rebounds all balls. When players miss a shot, they can take a "chance" and shoot again. Any time a shot is made, the player goes on to the next spot. When players miss a shot on the chance (the second shot), they have to switch places with their partner and must start over from the beginning when it becomes their turn. Challenge the students to see how many shots they can make in a row! *How far around can you go?*

Reminder
There may be more than two people shooting a basketball, so remind your students to be courteous to others by not shooting at the same time.

Pick a Shot

Each child partners up and decides who goes first. The shooter's partner rebounds all balls. The shooters from each pair choose a spot from anywhere within the boundaries to shoot. When shooters make their shots, they select another spot to shoot from. If they miss, they simply give the ball to their partner and rebound the shots. Encourage children to try to take some short and long shots.

Basketball Skills (3-5)

Objective

To improve basketball dribbling, shooting, guarding, and passing skills at various basketball stations.

Equipment

- ■ Basketballs (20) (If available, different colored balls at each station really help students distinguish which balls go where.)
- ■ Basketball goals (6) (Wall-mounted brackets for the side goals work great! These brackets hold rims that can be removed after use. If not enough goals are available, use big garbage cans.)
- ■ Traffic cones (to section off each station)

Procedure

Demonstrate each activity station (rules and how to play). Divide students into equal groups to play at each station. Choose from the following list which stations will work best for you, and eliminate or add stations to complement your class size or available equipment. See Basketball Skills layout on page 12 for setup.

Games and Activities

- ■ Dribbling or One-on-One: Students either practice ball-handling skills on their own, or they partner up and play Keep-Away. Make sure you take a moment to introduce or reinforce the walking and double-dribbling rules.
- ■ Chest or Bounce Pass: Students practice the chest and bounce pass to one another. To show them where to stand, place poly spots on the ground. Look for these things: (1) "squishing the bug," taking a step toward the person being passed to, (2) pushing from the chest, (3) good follow-through, with arms extended toward partner, hands out, and thumbs down.
- ■ Gotcha Tournament
- ■ Scoot 'n' Shoot
- ■ Spot Shot
- ■ Copycat
- ■ Pick a Shot

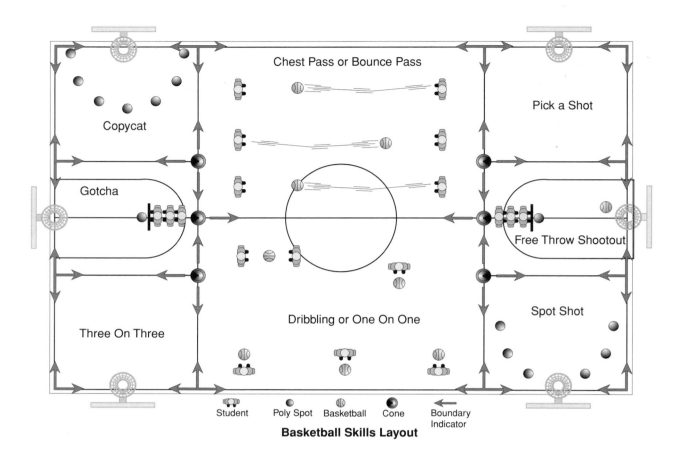

Basketball Skills Layout

Two Bounce

Students partner up and decide who goes first. The shooting partner from each group chooses a spot from anywhere within the boundaries to shoot. When the shooters make their shot, they simply select a new location to shoot from. The partners must be ready at all times, though, because when the shooters miss, they must quickly catch the missed shot before it bounces more than two times. The new shooter now shoots from the exact point where the ball made its first or second bounce, and the partner stays ready and waits for a missed shot. Note: If the ball is not caught after the second bounce, the ball gets returned to the shooter for a shot from a new spot. Continue this process until it is time to rotate.

Three-on-Three

Students play a game of man-to-man offense and defense, kind of like a mini-basketball game. After a shot has been made, teams switch sides by taking the ball back behind a predetermined line.

 Reminder

Introduce the overhead, crossover, or any other passes later on in the week.

Basketball and Frisbee Skills (P-5)

Objective

To develop, improve, and demonstrate the various skills of dribbling and shooting a basketball, one-on-one basketball, weave dribbling, the chest and bounce pass, throwing to a target, and throwing and catching a Frisbee.

Equipment

- Poly spots (40-50)
- Foam Frisbees (24-30)
- Traffic cones (to section off each station)
- Hula hoops (20-30)
- Basketballs (12-16)
- Five-gallon buckets (6-8)

Procedure

Demonstrate each activity station (rules and how to play). Divide students into equal groups to play at each station. Choose from the following list which stations work best for you, and eliminate or add stations to complement your class size or available equipment. See Basketball and Frisbee Skills layout for setup.

Games and Activities

- Weave Dribbling: Students form three or four lines and take turns moving in and out of the poly spots while dribbling a basketball.
- Frisbee Throw-and-Catch (with a partner): Students spread out with a partner. Give a brief demonstration of how to throw and catch a Frisbee, then have students take turns throwing and catching.

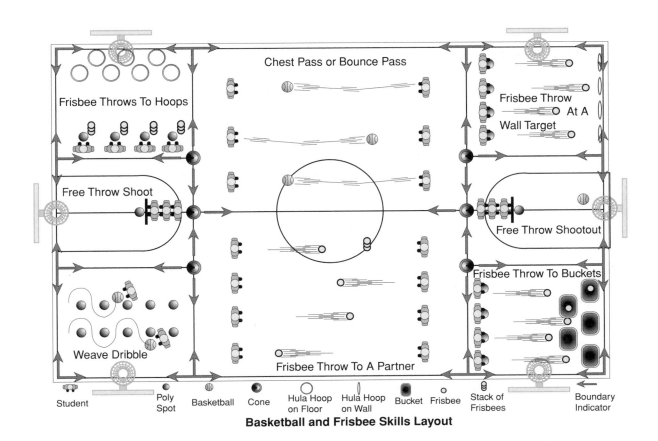

Basketball and Frisbee Skills Layout

■ Frisbee Throws to Hoops: Set out 10 to 15 hula hoops on the floor. Set out four to six poly spots about 5 to 10 yards away from hoops with three or four Frisbees at each spot (this is where students throw from). Once the students throw all of their Frisbees, they have to quickly but carefully retrieve them and take them back to their spot. Remind students to watch out for flying Frisbees. Before you have them begin the game, give them a brief demonstration of how to grip and throw a Frisbee. *How many Frisbees can you make into the hula hoops?*

■ Frisbee Throws to Buckets: Set out six to eight five-gallon buckets about 5 to 10 yards away from where you place four to six poly spots. Place three or four Frisbees at each spot. Once the students throw the three or four Frisbees, they must quickly but carefully retrieve them and take them back to their spot.

■ Frisbee Throws at a Wall Target: Tape five or six hula hoops on the wall about 5 to 10 yards away from where the students throw from. Set out four to six poly spots with three to four Frisbees at each spot. *Can you throw a Frisbee into each one of the hula hoops?*

■ Chest or Bounce Pass: Children practice the chest and bounce pass to one another. Place poly spots on the ground to show them where to stand. Look for these things: (1) "squishing the bug," or taking a step toward the person being passed to, (2) pushing from the chest, (3) good follow-through with arms extended toward partner, hands out, and thumbs down.

■ Frisbee Frenzy

■ Gotcha Tournament

■ Scoot 'n' Shoot

■ Copycat

Bowling, Frisbee, and Variety Stations (P-2)

Objective

To introduce and learn specific skills of bowling, such as how to hold and roll a bowling ball, aiming at bowling pins, and pin setup. Students also learn the putting skills of golf, such as how to grip and hold a putter and how to putt to a hole while on a putting green. Frisbee and Grab the Flag were selected as additional stations to maximize participation.

Equipment

■ Traffic cones (to section off each station and designate bowling lanes)

■ Putting greens and putters (3 or 4)

■ Golf balls per putting green (2 or 3)

■ Hula hoops (10-15) or Frisbee golf targets (4-6)

■ Bowling pins (32-40)

■ Rubber bowling balls or Gatorskin balls (4)

■ Foam Frisbees (24-30)

■ Foam noodles (6-8)

■ Yarn balls (100) in one trashcan

Procedure

Demonstrate each activity station (rules and how to play). Divide students into equal groups to play at each station. Choose from the following list which stations work best for you, and eliminate or add stations to complement your class size or available equipment.

Games and Activities

- Bowling: Designate two bowling lanes. Place the bowling lanes at each end of the gym so that students can use the wall as a barrier. Use traffic cones or border patrol to designate the boundary for the other side of the lane. Set up 8 to 10 pins in each corner of the gym (any way the teacher or students choose), which makes two lanes at each station. For example, if there are six children at station A, three bowl and set up pins  for one side while the other three bowl and set up for their side. Demonstrate to the students, proper grip, footwork, and aim for bowling. Each child is allowed two rolls (unless they get a strike). Avoid teaching how to score at the beginning of this unit. What is more important is to teach each child how to bowl the ball and how to experience a little success.

- Noodles: Set noodles out and challenge students to manipulate the noodle any way they can imagine.

- Frisbee Throw-and-Catch (with a partner): Students spread out with a partner. Give a brief demonstration of how to throw and catch a Frisbee, then have the students take turns throwing and catching.

- Putting Greens: Demonstrate how to grip the putter, how to stand, and how to aim at the cup when hitting the golf ball. Place two or three golf balls at each putting green, and instruct each child to hit each ball until it goes in the hole. When finished, children must retrieve their golf balls and hand them to the next person in line. If only two to four putting greens are available, have children hula hoop (or some other activity) while they wait their turn. *How many holes in one can you make?*

- Frisbee Throw to a Floor or Standing Target: Set out 10 to 15 hula hoops or four to six standing targets (like those used in Frisbee golf) about 5 to 10 yards away from where the students will be throwing from. Set out four to six poly spots with three or four Frisbees at each spot. Give a brief demonstration of grip and how to throw a Frisbee, then have them practice throwing the Frisbee to the hoops or targets. *How many Frisbees can you make into the hula hoops?*

- Aim and Bowl: Place four to six poly spots on the ground and near the wall, about five feet apart from each other. Set up two or three bowling pins on each spot, and set out four to six poly spots 5 to 10 yards away from bowling pins with one bowling ball or softball at each spot. Students work on accuracy by attempting to bowl the ball from their designated spots to knock down their pins. After each attempt, students must go set up pins and start over.

- Bowling Bombs

- Cross Over Craze

- Pin Bombardment

Trash It

Spread out all yarn balls inside the station boundaries. Place trashcan at the point furthest from the majority of the balls. The object of the game is for each student to pick up one yarn ball at a time and from that spot, toss it into the trashcan. Challenge students to see if they can get all the balls in the trashcan before it is time to rotate. After they rotate, dump and spread out all balls to start over with the next group.

VARIATION

To increase the time it takes to get all yarn balls into trashcans, increase the boundaries, place all players on scooters (if enough scooters are available), and add more trashcans. This game works great as a large-group, teamwork activity. Simply spread the yarn balls all over the gym, and time them to see how long it takes the class to get the yarn balls into the trashcans. Remember that once a yarn ball is picked up, a player cannot advance. Encourage students to pass the yarn balls to each other to get them into the trashcans as quickly as possible.

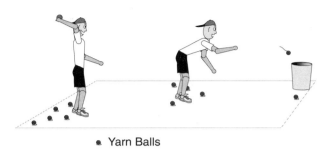

• Yarn Balls

Football and Frisbee Skills (3-5)

Objective

To develop throwing and catching techniques with a Frisbee and to learn the basic sport skills of football.

Equipment

- Traffic cones (to section off each station)
- Frisbees (20-30)
- Hula hoops and footballs (20-25)
- Large outdoor area (to avoid anyone from getting hit by a ball or Frisbee)

Procedure

Demonstrate each activity station (rules and how to play). Divide students into equal groups to play at each station. Choose from the following list which stations work best for you, and eliminate or add stations to complement your class size or available equipment. See Football and Frisbee Skills layout for setup on page 17.

Rules and Safety

- Stay in designated boundaries.
- Stay clear of Frisbee and football throwers as well as the kicking area.

Games and Activities

- Kicking Off a Tee: Place six to eight kicking tees so that no balls can be kicked into any of the other stations.
- Frisbee Throws to a Target: Set out 10 to 20 hula hoops about 15 to 20 yards away from where the students will be throwing. Set out 6 to 10 hoops with three or four Frisbees in each hoop (which is where the students will throw from). Once the students throw the three or four Frisbees, have them quickly but carefully retrieve them and take them back to their hoop. Give a brief demonstration of grip and how to throw a Frisbee before starting the game.
- Frisbee Throw-and-Catch (with a partner): Give a brief demonstration of how to catch a Frisbee. Afterward, have students spread out with a partner and take turns throwing and catching.

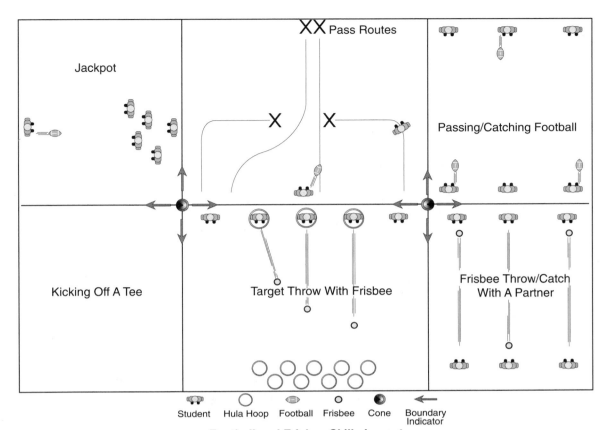

Football and Frisbee Skills Layout

- ■ Passing and Catching a Football: Give a brief demonstration of how to throw and catch a football. Students then spread out with a partner and take turns throwing and catching.
- ■ Pass Routes: Draw pass routes on cards, poster board, or on the ground to help students picture what routes to perform. Partners then take turns being the quarterback and the receiver (the quarterback picks the route per play). When the quarterback says "go," the receiver must run the route and catch the ball thrown by the quarterback. Have students switch positions after each play.
- ■ Flag Football
- ■ Keep Away
- ■ Grab the Flag
- ■ Frisbee Frenzy
- ■ In the Zone
- ■ Scooter Football

Jackpot

One person is the quarterback, and everyone else in the group stands approximately 15 yards away. The quarterback calls out "100," "200," "300," or "Jackpot." After calling out the points, the quarterback throws the ball high up in the air toward the group. Each student tries to catch the ball. A catch equals the number of points called out by the quarterback. If it is not caught in the air, no points are awarded. The first person to get to 500 points or the person who catches it when "Jackpot" is called wins! The winner then gets to be the quarterback. If the groups are too big for just one game at this station, separate them into two separate games (or however many necessary).

Reminder

Rotate about every five minutes counterclockwise on teacher's signal. Remind students that each station contains at least one hula hoop and that they must place Frisbees and balls in it before rotating.

Soccer Skills (P-5)

Objective

To perform kicking, trapping, dribbling, and passing skills during soccer stations to prepare them for a game-type situation. See Soccer Skills layout for setup.

Equipment

- Soccer or Nerf balls (35-40) (If possible, designate stations per colored balls to help eliminate confusion in the event that a ball is accidentally kicked out of a station.)
- Soccer goals (3 or 4)
- Poly spots (40-50)
- Traffic cones to section off each station
- Hula hoops are necessary at some stations. Students can place the balls in them before they rotate.

Procedure

Give a brief demonstration of each skill station. Remind all students that the first whistle means to get ready to rotate. Students get ready by cleaning their station for the next group. The second

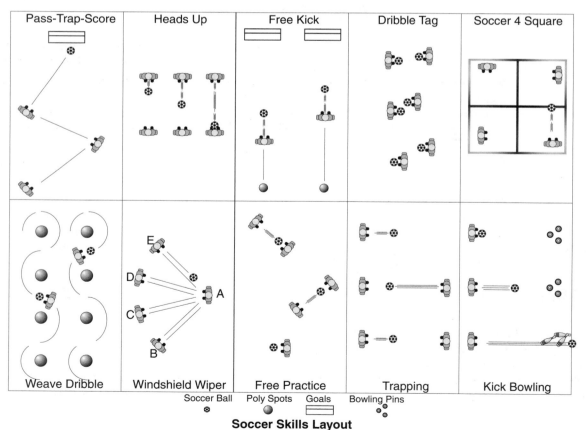

Soccer Skills Layout

whistle means to rotate. Also, consider your class size and the equipment or space available when selecting and adding new stations from the following activities.

Games and Activities

- Pass-Trap-Score: Set up one goal against the wall. The object of this station is for the students to use passing, trapping, and scoring together to score a goal. The first person (A) in line passes the ball to the trapping person (B), who passes it to the third person (C), who then controls the ball and shoots to score at the goal. A then rotates to B; B to C; and C to the front of the line (see Soccer Skills layout on page 18).

- Heads-Up: Students group themselves in pairs, with each pair having a ball. Standing no more than five feet apart, students take turns gently tossing the ball to each other in a way that their partner can head the ball. Remind them to keep their necks tense when they contact the ball at the forehead!

- Shot on Goal: Set up two or three goals against the wall and place a poly spot on the ground approximately 10 yards away from the goal. Starting from the poly spots, students dribble their soccer ball a short distance, then free kick it into the goal. Consider inserting a goalie to add more excitement to this station.

- Dribble Tag: For this station, give each student a soccer ball (if feasible). The object is for students to dribble and keep control of ball while at the same time trying to steal another student's ball.

- Dribble Weave: Students dribble a soccer ball with their feet while weaving in and out of the poly spots.

- Windshield Wiper: Students stand as demonstrated in Soccer Skills layout on page 18. Student A kicks the ball to student B. Student B traps the ball with a foot, then kicks it back to student A. Student A traps the ball using a foot, then passes it to student C. This process continues until student A has passed to everyone; afterward, everyone rotates one spot.

- Trapping: Students pair up, with each pair taking turns kicking or tossing the ball to one another. The methods of trapping (thigh, chest, and feet) that students practice depend on their age group.

- Kick Bowling: Set up three or four bowling pins on poly spots. Students work on accuracy by attempting to knock down the pins by kicking the ball from designated spots with either the inside or the outside of their foot. After each attempt, students should set up their pins on the designated spots and start over.

- Throw Ins: Students stand approximately 10 yards away from their partners (on spots) and practice making overhead tosses back and forth. Emphasize throwing for accuracy.

- Indoor Soccer

- Scooter Team Handball

Soccer Four-Square

Students play Four-Square using a soccer ball. The object is for students to move the ball from within the squares by passing and trapping and to keep the ball from going outside any of the squares. Four to six players may play from inside the Four-Square.

Dog Catcher

Students practice their dribbling skills on their own. One child, known as the "Dog Catcher," does not have a ball and must try to steal one away from someone in his or her group. The person it is stolen from is now the new Dog Catcher.

Target Practice (P-5)

Objective

To develop and improve aim and accuracy while manipulating a Frisbee, ball, or ring.

Equipment

- Freestanding Frisbee golf targets (9) or similar equipment to throw through (if these are not available, tape hula hoops on the wall as targets).
- Foam Frisbees (18-30)
- Soccer or hockey goals (3)
- Empty five-gallon buckets (6-8)
- Gatorskin balls (3-6)
- Juggling rings (for ring toss) (12-24)
- Traffic cones (to section off each station)
- Poly spots (to mark where to throw)
- Jump ropes (6-8) (to add an extra station, if necessary)
- Hula hoops (10-15)
- Yarn balls (24-36)

Procedure

The teacher demonstrates each activity station (rules and how to play) as well as the proper mechanics for holding and throwing a Frisbee and ball. Students are then divided into equal

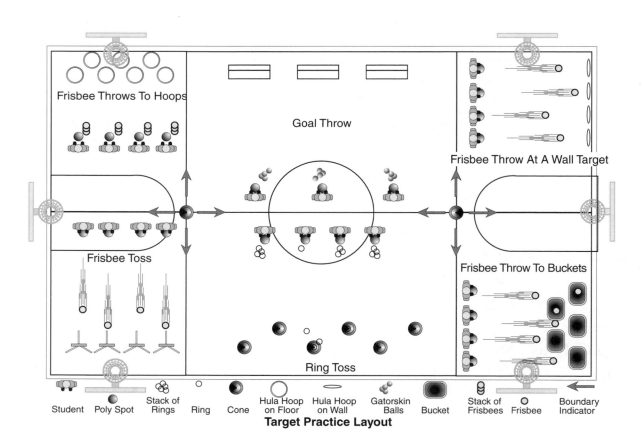

Target Practice Layout

groups to play at each station. Choose from the following list which stations work best for you. Remember to consider class size and available equipment when adding or eliminating stations. See Target Practice layout on page 20 for setup.

Games and Activities

- Frisbee Throw to a Standing Target: Students attempt to throw their foam Frisbees through one of the three or four standing targets. Set out three or four poly spots (which is where the students throw from) with three or four Frisbees at each spot. Once the students throw the foam Frisbees, instruct them to quickly but carefully retrieve them and take them back to their spot. Give a brief demonstration of grip and how to throw a Frisbee before starting the game. *How many Frisbees can you throw through the target?*

- Frisbee Throws to Hoops: Set out 10 to 15 hula hoops about 5 to 10 yards away from where the students will be throwing. Set out three or four poly spots with three or four foam Frisbees at each spot. Instruct the students to throw the foam Frisbees from the designated spots. After they have all been thrown, tell them to quickly but carefully retrieve the Frisbees and take them back to their spot. Before you begin the game, give the students a brief demonstration of grip and how to throw a Frisbee. *How many Frisbees can you make into the hula hoops?*

- Bucket Toss: Set out three or four five-gallon buckets about 5 to 10 yards away from where the students will be throwing. Set out four to six poly spots with three or four yarn balls at each spot. Have the students throw the yarn balls from the designated spots. After they do so, instruct them to quickly but carefully retrieve them to take them back to the original spots. *How many yarn balls can you make into the buckets?*

- Frisbee Toss: This station is the same as Bucket Toss, but use Frisbees instead of yarn balls.

- Ring Toss: Place four to six batting tees or traffic cones against a wall. Set out four to six poly spots with three or four juggling rings at each spot (this is where students toss from). Have the students grasp and toss the ring in a way that is similar to holding and throwing a Frisbee. The objective is to toss the ring on any of the tees or cones. *How many rings can you get onto the tees or cones?*

- Goal Throw: Place three soccer or hockey goals against the wall about 5 to 10 yards away from where the students will be throwing. Set out three or four poly spots with two or three Gatorskin balls at each spot. Standing in on the poly spots, the students see how many balls they can throw into this large target.

- Frisbee Throws at a Wall Target: Tape five or six hula hoops on the wall, about 5 to 10 yards away from where the students are throwing. Set out four to six poly spots with three or four foam Frisbees at each spot. Have the students stand on the poly spots and attempt to throw the Frisbees inside of the hula hoops.

- Bowling Bombs
- Cross Over Craze
- Dr. Feelgood
- Frisbee Frenzy
- Gator Bait
- In the Zone
- Pin Bombardment
- Swamp Ball
- Scooter Team Handball
- Team Trashball
- Toxic Blast

Body Awareness and Movement Exploration

Understanding and creating an awareness of our body and its relationship to people, places, and things is a prerequisite to skill acquisition in physical education. The following activities introduce balance, spatial awareness, and controlled movement.

Body Awareness (P-5)

Objective

To introduce spatial awareness and explore numerous ways of how and where the body can move in it.

Equipment

A gymnasium or large, open area

Procedure

To start class and perform the day's activities, do the 10-second countdown while directing each child to quickly sit down in personal space and get quiet before the countdown is up. Choose from the following "Games and Activities" which ideas will work best for you and your class. This list is not exhaustive, and you may want to eliminate ideas or add new ones, depending on the class objective.

Games and Activities

- Parts Together: Call out a number along with a particular body part. For example, call out "four and shoulder to shoulder." Four students then group together, touching shoulder to shoulder. Remind students that listening is very important to being successful in this activity.

- Exploring Body Shapes: Teach one body shape and see if they can give its opposite.
  - Narrow-wide, small-large, short-tall, curved, twisted, crooked, flat, pointed, and so on.
  - Combine with low, medium, and high levels.
  - *Can you make a bridge with your body? On four body parts only? Three body parts? Two?*
  - When the music begins, have the students move around the room. When it stops, instruct them freeze into the body shape, level, bridge, or a combination (teacher's choice).

- Effort: Ask children to mimic things in nature that represent the following concepts.
  - Time—Ask students to give examples of animals that are fast and slow. Instruct students to move around the room, pretending to move like the animals they mentioned.
  - Force—What elements in nature have strong or light forces? For example, lightning has a strong force, and a leaf falling to the ground has a light force. Instruct students to move around the room, pretending to make the forces they gave examples of.

- Flow: Again, give examples so that students understand the meanings of bound and free. For example, have them pretend to be bound in a puddle of glue. *How would you move in the glue? Now pretend you are a feather freely blowing in the wind.*

- Relationships With Others or to Objects: Spread out hula hoops. Instruct students to partner up and sit inside a hula hoop. Challenge partners by calling out one of the terms from the list to see if they can perform it and its opposite. Be creative! For example, have groups run inside the hoop, outside, or one inside and one outside. Have them also travel over, under, and through the hoop.

- ❏ In front and behind
- ❏ Inside and outside
- ❏ On and off
- ❏ Across
- ❏ Over, under, and through
- ❏ Leading and following
- ❏ Mirroring and shadowing

■ Locomotor Movement Themes: These activities help children to explore movement, and you can teach the following skills in progression. Randomly select children to demonstrate each skill. Instruct them then to think of an animal or creature that moves this way and to perform that movement while playing music.

- ❏ Creeping—Move one hand and elbow slowly after another (kind of like an army crawl). Move forward, backward, slowly, and as quickly as possible.
- ❏ Crawling—Move only on hands and knees at a medium level forward, backward, slowly and as quickly as possible. (Ask questions such as, "Can you crawl under things, over things?")
- ❏ Sliding along the floor—Move whole body in as low as a position as possible. Move on belly, seat, back, and in different directions.
- ❏ Walking—Walk forward as quickly as possible. Walk backward as quickly as possible.
- ❏ Crab Walk—Sit down with belly facing the ceiling. Now move around the gym with only hands and feet touching the floor. Move forward, backward, slowly, and as quick as possible.
- ❏ Bear Crawl—Sit down with belly facing the floor. Now move around the gym with only hands and feet touching the floor. Move forward, backward, slowly, and as quickly as possible.
- ❏ Marching—Pretend you are in a marching band. Make sure to raise your knees to waist level. Move forward, backward, slowly, and as quickly as possible.
- ❏ Hopping—Spring from one foot, and land on that same foot. Move forward and backward.
- ❏ Jumping—Push off both feet, and land on both feet. Move forward and backward.
- ❏ Hopscotch—Push off both feet, then land on one foot; push off one foot then land back on both feet. Hop, jump, hop, jump, and so on.
- ❏ Galloping—Make a forward movement with one foot leading and the other foot following (kind of like follow the leader). Move forward, backward, slowly, and as quickly as possible.
- ❏ Slide-Step—Step sideways with either foot. The other foot quickly follows, like galloping, but sideways. Move to the right, left, and across the room, changing directions.
- ❏ Skipping—Do a series of "step-hops." Step forward with one foot, perform a small hop on that same foot, then perform the same action with the other foot. Move forward, backward, and in different directions.
- ❏ Directions, Levels, and Pathways—Have the students perform locomotor movements while moving forward, backward, sideways, diagonal, up or down, right or left, and clockwise or counterclockwise in straight, curved, or zigzag lines at low, medium, or high levels.

■ Nonlocomotor Movements

- ❏ Bending—Perform movement at a joint (this increases flexibility and range of motion). Bend body parts fast and slow, down and up, forward and backward, left and right.

❏ Rocking—Move balance from one spot to another. *Show ways that you can you rock on your tummy or back.*

❏ Swinging—Action of body parts that resemble swinging motions: a rope swinging, a pendulum of a clock swinging, an elephant swinging its trunk. Swing arms with a partner.

❏ Turning—Turn the body as a whole. Keep your balance. Turn your body around. Stand on one foot, and turn on the balls of your feet. Lie on your belly or back, and turn around. Do a partner turnaround.

❏ Twisting—While on the floor, twist your upper body, one body part, or two body parts.

❏ Pushing—Partner up, face each other, and form a bridge by locking hands and leaning toward the middle. *Who can push the other person backward?*

❏ Backward Pushing—Now get on your backs and form a bridge by pushing your feet against your partner's feet. *Who can push the other person backward?*

❏ Pulling—Partner up, face each other, and lock hands. Now play human tug-of-war. *Can you invent a new way of pulling to demonstrate for us?*

Busy Bee

This game reviews comprehension of the various body parts. Students move around the room (any way the teacher prescribes) to upbeat music. When the music stops, the teacher calls out a body part. Children must then quickly find someone and touch that particular body part on their partners. For example, elbows to elbows, nose to nose, fingers to ribs, and so on. Be creative with this game!

Alphabet Mania

This game enhances letter recognition and helps students explore pathways. Spread poly spots with alphabet letters written on the back of them all over the gym. Once students partner up, give them one jump rope (beaded ropes work best), and on the signal, have them travel around the room in a chosen locomotor movement. When the stop signal is given, the students have to search for a poly spot, turn it over, and then make the letter with the jump rope on the ground. The teacher circulates, asks students what various pathways their letter has in it, and then begins the game again.

Gymnastics (P-2)

An excellent way to begin this subunit is to contact your local gymnastics club. Call a month or two in advance to request a demonstration of a team performance or two days of trained instructors teaching gymnastics stations. Local clubs are usually interested in doing this type of work because it brings in new business. If possible, make sure to request that the clubs send both girls and boys to demonstrate skills. After students observe the gymnastics performance, they often become excited and motivated to get started with this unit.

Objective

To participate in playful gymnastics activities to build muscular strength and endurance, flexibility, balance, posture, creative expression, and overall coordination.

Equipment

Gymnastics mats (10-12), spread out all over the gym

Procedure

Divide students into equal groups, and assign each group one mat. The teacher either demonstrates the skills or chooses those proficient enough to assist in demonstrating each skill properly and safely. After the following "Rules and Safety" section is a list that includes balances, stunts, tumbling drills, and partner stunts from which you can build your stations. Remember, consider your class size and the equipment or space available when you add ideas or modify existing activities.

Rules and Safety

- Stay on your assigned mat unless told otherwise.
- Always use a spotter on the particular skills instructed by the teacher.
- Never place any pressure on your head!
- On balance stunts, always position yourself so that if you fall, you will land on the mat.
- When performing any tumbles, make sure there is only one person at a time on the mat.

Games and Activities

- Stork Stand: Balance on one foot with hands tucked in like a storks feathers. *Now try balancing on the other foot. Now spin around in circles, but when I say "stop," get back into a stork balance. Now spin around in circles again, but this time, get in your stork stand with your eyes closed. Can you stay balanced with your eyes closed?*
- Airplane Balance: Arms out, lean over with one leg back, now one leg forward, now to the side, now try combinations using all of these. *Remember, it is not how fast you do them; it is how well you stay balanced.*

- No-Hands Sit-Stand: Stand with feet shoulder-width apart and arms out front. Sit down and then stand up without crossing legs, placing hands on the floor, or kneeling.
- Finger Touch: Stand with feet shoulder-width apart and one hand behind you with pointer finger pointed down. Reach around and grab your wrist. *Now can you squat down and touch the floor with your pointer finger?*
- Toe to Nose: While standing, grab and lift one foot slowly without falling over. Try to touch your foot to your nose or forehead and then place your foot back down.
- Thread the Needle: Stand, join hands (interlocking fingers) in front of you. Now try to step through your clasped hands with one leg (do not let go of your fingers) then through the other leg while maintaining your balance. Your arms should now be behind you. *Can you get back to your starting position? Try this while lying down.*

- Knee Dip: While standing, reach behind you and grab your right foot with your left hand (or vice versa). *Can you squat down, touch your knee to the ground, and get back up without letting go or falling over?*
- Ankle Hold Stand-Up: Sit down with legs straight in front of you. *While grasping your right ankle with your right hand, can you stand while still holding your ankle, but not using your other hand? Try the left side.*

- No-Hands Stand: Lie flat on your back. With one continuous motion, can you rock yourself up into a standing position without placing your hands on the ground? With arms folded at your chest?

- Corkscrew Stand: Stand with feet shoulder-width apart. Pivot and rotate on the balls of your feet a half-turn, crossing your legs and lowering yourself to the floor. Now stand up again.

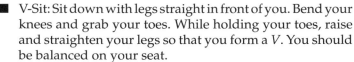

- V-Sit: Sit down with legs straight in front of you. Bend your knees and grab your toes. While holding your toes, raise and straighten your legs so that you form a *V*. You should be balanced on your seat.

- Shoulder Rest: Lie on your back and raise your feet as high as you can toward the ceiling with just your upper back and shoulders touching the floor. Place your hands at your hips to support your body.

- Bridges: *Can you make a bridge with your body? How many different bridges can you make (tall, narrow, low, wide)? Can you make a bridge on two hands, one foot; two feet, one hand; one foot, one hand?*

Tumbling

Each group forms a line on one end and performs each skill. Only one child on the mat at a time!

! Reminder

There are many methods to teaching tumbling skills. It is recommended that you get up-to-date teaching resources or speak with a local gymnastics instructor on the proper safety of the following tumbling skills. Again, remind children to never roll with pressure on their head. If they feel pressure or if their neck is getting sore, they should stop immediately! Also, for safety precautions, always use a spotter.

- Lame Dog: Walk down the mat on your right hand and left foot, or vice versa.

- Knee Walk: Kneel down on your knees, grab your feet, and move down the mat by walking on your knees.

- Walrus Walk: Get into push-up position. Move down the mat as if your legs were limp, walking only with your hands and dragging your feet behind you.

- Turtle Walk: Get as wide as you can, and walk down the mat slowly, like a huge turtle.

- Log Roll: Roll down the mat with your hands straight against your side. Roll like a log.

- Pencil Roll: Roll down the mat like a log, but with your hands pointed straight above your head, like a sharp pencil.

- Egg Roll: Lie down on the mat and ball up by hugging both your knees. Then roll like a wobbling egg.
- Forward Roll: Squat down with knees together. Place your hands on the floor outside of your knees, and tuck your chin to your chest. Roll forward, landing on the top of your shoulders while grabbing your shins to stay balled up as you roll to your feet.
- Back Roller: Use this tumble as a lead-up to the backward roll. Crouch down with your knees together and hands clasped behind your neck. Slowly fall backward, and rock back and forth.
- Back Curl: Use this activity as a lead-up to the backward roll. Perform this skill the same as the back roller, but this time after falling backward, attempt to whip the legs over to touch your feet to the floor behind you.
- Backward Roll, Hand-Clasped Position: Hands clasped behind neck, elbows out. From a crouched position, quickly fall backward. Whip your legs over to touch your feet to the floor, taking as much weight on the forearms as possible.
- Cartwheel: Stand sideways to mat with feet shoulder-width apart, and pretend you're a wheel about to roll. Remember to always keep your arms and legs perfectly straight throughout the cartwheel. Using a lot of momentum, place your left hand down, followed by your right hand as you whip your legs (spread apart) toward the ceiling. Land back on the mat with a straight right foot, followed by a straight left foot to stand upright.

Fun Stunts

- Seal: Lie on your belly with hands shoulder-width apart. Straighten your arms and curl your head and upper body back toward your feet. The lower half of your body should remain on the ground. Now bark like a seal. "Arf! Arf!"

- Birdbath: Perform the seal again, but this time bend your knees and try to curl your feet up to your head. *Can you touch your feet to your head?* This one takes lots of flexibility.
- Rocking Chair: Lie on your tummy and bend your knees. Now arch back, grasp your ankles and pull, rocking your body back and forth. *Are there other ways you can rock your body? On your back, side to side? Can you rock up to a stand?*

- 180 and 360: Stand with feet shoulder-width apart and try to jump high while twisting your body halfway around. Land back on your feet, facing the direction opposite from where you started. Try it again, but see if you can jump and twist *all* the way around. Land so that you are facing the direction you started at.
- Mad Cat: Get in push-up position. Keeping your hands still, slowly walk your feet up without bending your legs until they meet your hands (kind of like an angry cat). Then walk your hands up until you're back to the starting position.

■ Knee-Jump to Stand: Kneel down with knees on ground. Now swing your arms back and forth and propel yourself upward, landing on your feet.

■ Donkey Kick: Make a bridge facing down. Now with hands on the ground, kick your feet up in the air like a donkey. Make sure you can do the Donkey Kick before you try the cartwheel.

■ Jump Through: While standing, bend one leg in front of your body and grab your shoe. Your body should look like the number "4." Now jump through the hole that you have created. Bring the foot that is on the ground up and through the space created from grasping your foot, without letting go of your shoe. *Can you land back on your foot without letting go or falling over?*

Partner Stunts

■ Wring the Dishcloth: Partners stand facing each other and holding hands. Raise one pair of arms, turning together under those arms resulting in a back-to-back position, still holding arms. Raise the other pair of arms, turning together under those arms to end facing each other. *Can you do this in one continuous motion? Can you reverse directions?*

■ Double Stand Back-to-Back: Partners sit back-to-back and lock elbows. While pushing against each other's backs, stand up together, then go back down.

■ Double Stand Face-to-Face: Partners sit facing each other with knees bent and toes touching each other's. Grab partner's hands, and at the same time, pull backward to bring yourselves to a standing position, then go back down.

■ Leapfrog: One partner (the rock) crouches on knees, head down, with arms over the head for protection. The other partner (the frog) jumps over the rock.

■ Archway: Partners lie down with their heads touching, but in a straight line. Children then perform a shoulder rest, attempting to get their feet to touch, forming an archway.

■ Over the Fence: Shake hands with your partner (right hand to right hand). Now partner A swings the left leg over the joined hands to straddle partner B's arm so that partner A's back is to partner B's front. Partner B then swings the left leg over as well, so that partner B's back is to partner A's back.

Partner A continues with the right leg, then partner B takes a turn until both are back at their starting positions without letting go of each other's hands. *How fast can you do it?*

■ Partner Two-Step: Partner A steps onto partner B's feet, with each partner's hands resting on each other's shoulders. When partner B lifts the right foot, partner A lifts the left foot so that partner B is not actually picking up both partners' feet. Continue this while playing some music, and make sure they switch roles.

■ See Saw: Partners sit with knees bent, facing each other, but for this one to be successful, students have to sit on each other's feet. While holding onto each other's shoulders, or by grabbing each other's hands, begin rocking back and forward, like being on a seesaw.

■ Partner Hopping, Facing Each Other: Stand facing each other with each partner's right leg extended to the other. Each partner then grabs the other partner's ankle with the left hand. Next, reach across, shake hands, and begin hopping together, each on your one foot. Remember to keep legs straight.

■ Partner Hopping, Side by Side: Stand side by side, and place your inside arms around each other's shoulders. Then reach down with your outside hands to grab your inside ankles, pulling your inside legs behind you. With only the outside foot of each partner down, begin hopping side by side.

■ Hitching a Ride: Partner A gets down on all fours, and partner B gets on partner A, as if getting on a horse backwards. Once on partner A's back, partner B leans forward, grabbing on to partner A's ankles to go for a ride. Switch roles.

■ Centipede: Partners A and B each get down on all fours, one directly in front of the other. Partner B then places both feet on the shoulders of partner A who is directly behind him (knees should be off the ground). Now begin to move around the room. *How many people can you add to your centipede?*

Gymnastics (3-5)

Provide this station format to reinforce and enhance previously learned information (pages 24-29). Have the children participate at the various gymnastics stations, and allocate no more than a week to conduct this unit.

Objective

To demonstrate an understanding of balances, stunts, tumbling, and partner stunts.

Procedure

Divide students into equal groups, and assign each group one mat. The teacher either demonstrates the skills or chooses those proficient enough to assist in demonstrating each skill properly and safely.

Equipment

Gymnastics mats (10-12) (spread out all over the gym)

Rules and Safety

- Stay on your assigned mat, unless told otherwise.
- Remember that safety is the most important skill to practice.
- Always use a spotter, as instructed by the teacher.
- Before every stunt, pay attention to the demonstration by the teacher or student.
- On balance stunts, always position yourself so that if you fall, you land on the mat.
- When performing any tumbles, remember—one person on the mat at a time.
- No horseplay.
- Never place any pressure on your head.

Tumbling

Each group forms a line on one end and performs each skill. Only one child on the mat at a time! You may want to begin with the tumbling skills from the P-2 unit on pages 26-27.

- Egg Roll
- Log Roll
- Walrus Walk
- Knee Walk
- Forward Roll
- Judo Roll
- Forward Roll (to a straddle and from a straddle)
- Cartwheel
- Front Round-off
- Churn-the-Butter: In push-up position with the body stiff, lift one arm and leg (both from the same side) and roll over into a face-up position. Remember, the body must remain stiff, and only your hands and feet should be touching the floor. Now lift the other arm and leg, and roll back to a push-up position. Continue this pattern all the way down the mat.

Balance Stunts

- Tripod Balance on Forehead (use spotters)
- Frog Stand (two-point stand)
- Tripod-to-Headstand (use spotters)

Partner/Group Balance Stunts

- Air Chair

- Lean 2

- V-Stand

- Face-to-Face (see P-2 unit)
- Back-to-Back (see P-2 unit)
- Centipede (see P-2 unit)

- Lazy Chair

- Cheerleader

■ Copycats

■ Bunk Beds

■ The Surfer

■ Lighthouse

■ Table Top

■ The Bridge

■ Firefighter Carry

■ Knee Stand

■ The Star

■ Platform Stand

■ Mountain Top

■ Trim the Hedge

■ The Fan

■ Millipede

■ Chariot

■ Invent Your Own

EXAMPLE

 Reminder

Depending on the stunt, foot placement must either be on lower back or hip joint. If a student's back is hurting, that student should be a spotter and not participate in the stunt.

 VARIATION

Try implementing the station format. The teacher demonstrates each activity station (rules and how to do each skill). Children are then divided into equal groups, and they rotate from station to station every four to five minutes. Choose from previously taught material which skills and stations work best for you, and remember to add or eliminate per class size and available equipment. Place posters on the walls at each station to remind children of what they are to do at each station. Posters may contain rules and safety, a description of each skill, or they may simply be visuals to clarify any previously learned skill they may have forgotten. Use traffic cones to section off each activity station.

Group Gymnastics Creations

This activity is optional, but your students will love it. Have all students form groups of at least four to six. Explain that each group is allowed the whole class period to create their own gymnastics routine. Each routine must include a combination of at least one previously learned balance stunt, tumbling skill, and partner or group stunt. Each group, if permitted, may choose a song to perform their routine to. Remind each group that they will be assessed on the following criteria:

1. Teams demonstrate originality and creativity.
2. Teamwork—everyone is involved and trying.
3. Each routine involves at least one skill from each area.

Immediately upon arriving for their next physical education class, students practice their routine during the first half of class and perform during the last half of class. Each group has the option to perform their routine with or without music.

Certificates or temporary trophies (again, this is optional) may be awarded to the top group, as chosen by the teacher or by student applause. Students demonstrating high levels of teamwork and leadership should also be rewarded with certificates.

Reminder

• *Make sure you do an after-school announcement recognizing these individuals.*

Paper Plate Skills (P-2)

Objective

To become proficient in both stationary and locomotor skills

Equipment

- ■ Paper plates (2 per child)
- ■ Music (any upbeat music that your students love moving to)

Procedure

Randomly scatter paper plates around the gym. Instruct students to get two paper plates, then to find their own personal space and stand on their plates. When everyone is ready, demonstrate the following cues. Call out the different skill cues while playing music. Remember there is no particular order, simply call out the skills or combine these skills into your own paper plate routine.

Skill Cues

- ■ Stationary Skills
    - ❑ Boxing: Punch up and down or forward.
    - ❑ Shake: Shake right, left, up, or down.
    - ❑ Tap: Tap body parts that are called out.
    - ❑ Clap: Clap with the paper plates.
    - ❑ Scrape: Scrape up and scrape down.
    - ❑ Twist: Twist on the plates.
    - ❑ Wax On, Wax Off: Take turns brushing your feet in circles.

- ❏ Scissors: While standing in place, slide one foot forward and one foot backward in an alternating, continuous motion.
- ❏ X-ercise: While standing in place, slide both feet apart then cross your feet (like an X) as you bring them back in.
- ❏ Spin Out: While standing in place, spin on one plate. *How many circles can you make before stopping?*
- ■ Locomotor Skills
  - ❏ Skating Forward: Pretend you are roller blading forward.
  - ❏ Skating Backward or Moonwalking: Pretend you are in-line skating backward or moonwalking like Michael Jackson.
  - ❏ Slide-Step: Slide-step right, then together with the left, and so on. Now go to your left.
  - ❏ Scooter: While standing, place the front foot on a plate and push yourself forward with the back foot. Hold the other plate in both hands and pretend to steer your car.
  - ❏ Snowplow: Place both hands on the plates and push forward with your feet.
  - ❏ Now make up your own paper-plate skill. (Teachers need to make sure to watch the students during this time. They may show you a new skill to add to the list.)
  - ❏ Partner up and do the skills as they are called out, or perform whatever skills you want to do.

Jump Rope Skills

An excellent way to begin this activity is to contact your local American Heart Association to request a *Jump Rope for Heart* demonstration team performance (call a month or two in advance). When children observe students their own age perform the wide array of challenging rope skills, they all of sudden become very excited and motivated to start jumping.

The American Heart Association has manuals, kits, and videos entitled *Jump Rope for Heart* that provide the most complete coverage of jump rope benefits, suggested approaches to teaching, and the how-tos of all skills. The manuals provide excellent approaches to single, partner, and long-rope skills with basic, intermediate, and advanced skill levels. Most importantly, the American Heart Association provides these resources for free. For information about ordering their *Jump Rope for Heart* kits for your school or organization, simply contact your local chapter or find them at **www.americanheart.org.**

Give students rules and information for their safety.

- Show students how to determine correct rope length.
- Instruct them to stay a safe distance away from other jumpers.
- Inform them that they must wear tennis shoes.
- Maintain proper spacing between groups.
- Stay in previously established groups.

Single-Rope Skills (P-2)

Objective

To demonstrate competency in single rope jumping skills, while also enhancing agility, coordination, rhythm, cardiovascular endurance, teamwork, and creativity skills.

Equipment

- Ropes (1 per child)
- Music

Procedure

Before the children arrive, spread out ropes all over the room. At the beginning of class, instruct children to select a rope and with it make a circle to stand in. This helps designate their personal space. Cover and follow a progression of jump rope skills based on the knowledge and abilities of the class. Provide the students with a few minutes of free jump at the beginning and end of every day to allow for warm-up and practice. Observe overall skill acquisition to determine progression of skills.

Games and Activities

- Go over general jumping hints.
- Help students establish a rhythm. For example: "One, two, turn, jump."
- Instruct children to make a smiley face with rope.
- Instruct students to perform a toe trap by turning the rope over their heads and lifting up the toes of one foot to trap the rope.
- Pretend to be an extremely "clueless" learner, and have the children teach you the how-tos of rope jumping. Note: Have them teach you all the basics from beginning to end, and then challenge them to practice what they just taught you.

Long-Rope Skills (P-2)

Objective

To demonstrate competency in long-rope jumping skills, while also enhancing agility, coordination, rhythm, cardiovascular endurance, teamwork, and creativity skills.

Equipment

- Rope (1 for every group)
- Music

Procedure

Divide students into groups of four to six and have them sit by a rope. Two children from each group get on each end to hold the rope. Make sure everyone gets a turn holding the rope. Follow a progression of skills based on overall skill acquisition of the class. Instruct them that when the teacher says "switch," turners and jumpers need to rotate positions. The turners become jumpers and the jumpers become turners. Remember to give them a few minutes of free jump at the end of every day.

Games and Activities

- Pretend your rope is a tightrope. Take turns walking forward, backward, and sideways on the rope, crossing one foot in front of the other, then behind the other.

- Form a bridge over the rope. Move your bridge up and down the rope. *What other ways can you move up and down the rope?*

- When the music turns on, run, skip, gallop, or hop. *Watch where you are going, and see how many ropes you can jump over before the music is turned off.*

- *Keeping your feet together, can you zigzag jump forward, backward, and up and down your rope? Can you zigzag forward or backward while hopping on one foot?*

- *Keeping your hands on the floor, can you jump back and forth across the rope? How fast or how high can you go?*

- Snake Bite: Rapidly wiggle each end of the rope from side to side along the ground (like a snake wiggling on the ground). Jumpers attempt to run and jump over the rope, then they return to the end of the line. *Don't get bit by the snake!*

- Tidal Waves: Make waves by rapidly raising and lowering each end of the rope along the ground. Jumpers attempt to run and jump over the rope, then they return to the end of the line. Gradually increase the size of the waves. *Don't get hit by the tidal wave!*

■ Climbing the Hill: One child sits down while holding the end of the rope on the floor. The other child stands up and pulls the rope tight, holding the rope at waist level. Starting at the bottom of the hill, each child runs and jumps over the rope, each time jumping higher and higher. Then, keeping their feet together, the children take turns jumping zigzag up the hill. *Can you go to the top without touching the rope?*

■ The Swing Jump: A great lead-up before the children actually turn the rope and jump. One child stands in the middle with the rope beside the feet. Turners gently swing the rope out together, repeating this motion from side to side. Each time the rope gets to the middle, the jumper jumps in place over the rope. *How many times can you swing jump before you touch the rope?*

■ Run Through: Rope turners slowly turn the rope. Each person, in a follow-the-leader pattern, tries to run through without getting hit by the rope.

VARIATIONS

As soon as students enter the gym, do not have them form groups. Simply allow children, as you call out the above skills, to perform the skills at any rope they choose while moving around the gym. This quickly gets everyone active and places the challenge and responsibility on each child.

Long rope skills provide a great opportunity to utilize fourth and fifth grade student teachers as turners, especially in pre-kindergarten and kindergarten. Teach a progression of the following skills based on overall comprehension of the majority of the class.

■ Single, Long-Rope Turning: Children simply practice turning—no jumping yet.

■ Single, Long-Rope Jumping (cold start): Jumper stands in middle. When rope turners say "ready, set, go," the jumper begins jumping as the rope comes down toward the feet.

■ Single Long-Rope, Entering Front Door: With the rope already turning, the jumper stands on the outside of the rope. On the downswing (head to toe), the jumper enters the middle and begins jumping.

■ Single Long-Rope, Entering Back Door: With the rope already turning, the jumper stands on the outside of the rope. On the upswing (toe to head), the jumper enters the middle and begins jumping.

■ Single Long-Rope: Practice exiting the rope.

Jump Rope Stations (P-2)

Objective

To enhance and improve jump rope and game skills at various activity stations.

Equipment

■ Long ropes (2)
■ Thundersticks (2)
■ Short ropes (16-20)
■ Flags, scooters, and hoops (8-10)
■ Colored jersey
■ Music
■ Traffic cones to section off each station

Procedure

The teacher demonstrates each activity station (rules and how to play), then divides children into equal groups to play at the following stations. Choose from the following list which stations work best for you. You may wish to eliminate or add stations based on class size and available equipment.

Games and Activities

- Single-Rope Skills (two stations): Write all single-rope skills on posters or task cards to remind children of the skills they can practice at this station.
- Long-Rope Skills: On posters, write down Snake Bite, Tidal Waves, Climbing the Hill, Swing Jump, and Front and Back Door Entry to remind children of the skills they can practice at this station.
- Grab the Flag: Each student gets a flag (flag belts work best). Have them tuck in their shirts and stuff the flag into their pockets or pants. Students must stay inside the designated boundaries. If a student steps outside the boundaries, with or without a flag, the student is out. To begin, each student tries to pull other players' flags by chasing them and pulling them out and dropping them to the ground. If a flag is pulled, a player must perform 10 to 15 repetitions of their favorite exercise (jumping jacks, for example) before returning to the game. Players cannot guard their flag to prevent others from pulling it. You can play boys vs. girls, certain colors flags vs. other colors, and so on.
- Scooter Chain Tag: Each child gets on a scooter with one being "It" (this child puts on the colored jersey). Everyone else tries to avoid the It, but each player must stay inside the coned-off area. If tagged, the player must connect with the It by grabbing the It's scooter handle or by locking arms with the It. Once connected to the chain of It, players can't let go and must use teamwork to move around. Have them continue this process until there is a complete chain. Start over with the last person getting tagged being the It.
- Run Through: Rope turners slowly turn the rope and each person, in a follow-the-leader pattern, tries to run through without getting hit by the rope.
- Hula Hoop: Everyone pick up a hula hoop. There must be enough equipment for everyone at each station. *Can you hula hoop until the signal is given to rotate?*
- Thunderstick: One child sits down with the thunderstick in between the two cones already set up. The object is to slide the thunderstick back and forth across the ground while the players (who must stay in their own spot) avoid the thunderstick by jumping over it. Players who get hit may jump rope until the next game. The last person standing gets to slide the thunderstick back and forth. Remember: do not raise the thunderstick off the ground!

Jump Rope Stations (3-5)

Objective

To cover and follow a progression of basic to advanced single-rope, partner, and long-rope skills based on the knowledge and overall abilities of the class.

Equipment

- Long ropes and thundersticks (2 each)
- Short ropes (16-20)
- Flags, scooters, and hoops (8-10)
- Music
- Traffic cones (to section off each station)

Procedure

The teacher demonstrates each activity station (rules and how to play). Divide the children into equal groups to play at the following stations. Choose from the following list the stations that will work best for you. Add or eliminate stations based on class size or equipment available.

Games and Activities

- Long-Rope Skills (with a ball and beanbag): While jumping, students (1) attempt to catch a thrown ball, (2) dribble or pass a basketball, (3) toss up and catch a beanbag, and (4) create a stunt.
- Partner Rope Challenges (two stations): Write all partner rope skills on posters or task cards to remind children of the skills they can practice at these stations.
- Short-Rope Challenges (two stations): Write all single-rope skills on posters or task cards to remind children of the skills they can practice at these stations.
- Scooter Chain Tag or Thunderstick: See P-2 stations.
- Whirlwind: See "Whirlwind Tournaments" in chapter 2 for rules and how to play (pages 114-115).
- Hula Hoop: Challenge the students to see how long they can hula hoop. *Can you hula hoop until the signal is given to rotate?*
- To jump a self-turned rope with a partner. To learn and perform two-in-one (two people, one rope) and two-in-two (two people, two ropes) to improve teamwork, cooperation, rhythm, coordination, and cardiovascular endurance.
- Instruct students to partner up. Follow a progression of skills based on the students' performance and comprehension. Review at the beginning of each class by having students demonstrate previously learned skills. Instruct students to create their own partner-jumps, and if time permits, allow "show-off" time to demonstrate some of their newly acquired skills.
- Assign four to six skippers per group, two to four jumpers and two turners. Each eventually alternates so that everyone gets a turn at each position. Follow a progression of skills based on students' performance and comprehension. Review at the beginning of class by having students demonstrate previously learned skills.

Group Routines (3-5)

Objective

To improve teamwork, cooperation, rhythm, coordination, and cardiovascular endurance.

Procedure

Students form groups of at least four to six. Explain that each group is allowed 20 minutes to create their own jump rope routine. Each routine must include a combination of at least one previously learned single, partner, and long-rope skill. During the last half of class, each group performs their routine for the class (with or without music). Let them know that groups are assessed using the following criteria:

1. Groups demonstrate originality and creativity.
2. Teamwork—everyone is involved and trying.
3. Each group's routine involves at least one skill from each area.

Certificates or a temporary trophy (again, this is optional) may be awarded to the top group as chosen by the teacher or student applause.

Miscellaneous Activities

These innovative, nontraditional activities are designed to broaden physical education's scope and strengthen the achievement of overall curriculum goals. They also introduce some skills that may lead to lifetime fitness interests.

Fitness for the Fun of It (P-5)

Objective

Fitness for the fun of it is an alternative form of past fitness tests without the task of giving the actual tests. These fitness stations provide a variety of challenging, invigorating, yet developmentally appropriate, activities to enhance muscular and cardiovascular strength and endurance, flexibility, agility, balance, coordination, and speed.

Equipment (P-2)

- Gymnastics mats (2-4)
- Juggling scarves (14-18)
- Beanbags (8-10)
- Four-Square ball (1)
- Hula hoops, flags/streamers, yarn balls, and jump ropes (6)
- Traffic cones (to section off each station and 6 for mountain climbers)
- Balancing objects (3-6)
- Hacky Sacks (2-3)

Procedure

Demonstrate all activity stations (rules and how to play) that the children will perform to improve health and skill-related fitness objectives. Divide students into equal groups, and rotate them from each station every one to two minutes. Choose from the following list which stations will work best for you. You may want to eliminate or add stations, depending on your class size or available equipment.

Games and Activities

- Cone Mountain Climbers: Place cones on their sides and have children jump (feet together) from the lowest to the highest point and back. Attempt this as many times as possible.
- Scarf Juggling: Challenge children to keep two or three scarves from touching the ground.
- Give and Grab: Children partner up and face each other. One child sits pretzel style, and one gets in the push-up position with two beanbags on the floor in front of each hand. On "go," the child in push-up position picks up a bean bag and places it in the partner's ex-  tended hand, then picks up the other bean bag and places it in the partner's other extended hand. Have the children continue this process 8 to 10 times, giving and grabbing the beanbags before switching positions. For added challenge have seated partners slowly raise their hands each time the beanbags are taken away.
- Hula Hoop: Challenge children to hula hoop as long as they can.
- Speed Ropes: Tell students to do as many jumps of the rope as they can.
- Run-Downs: Start the children at an end line. Challenge them to run down and touch the closest free throw line, then run back to the end line as many times as possible.
- Partner Sit-ups: Partners must lie down, with soles of feet together, knees bent. The object of this activity is for students to hand a beanbag to their partner between each sit-up. One sit-up by each student counts as one. Sit-ups that do not count include ones with dropped

or thrown beanbags, ones with elbows touching the ground, or ones that are incomplete. Challenge children to see how many they can do before it is time to rotate.

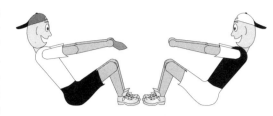

■ Macarena Push-Ups: Students get in push-up position and perform the Macarena hand movements while always balancing on one hand. Each hand should go to the following spots: hand, shoulders, neck, hips, and seat (then swivel hips three times and start over).

■ Balance Station: Set out various balancing equipment such as a Wobbler™, balance rope, and balance master. Challenge children to see how long they can balance.

Push-Up Hockey

Children partner up and face each other. Both are in the push-up position, facing each other about four to five feet apart (closer together as they get better). One child has a beanbag and tries to slide it through their partner's arms. The opposing partner reacts, attempting to block the beanbag from going through. One point is given for each score between the arms.

Quick Feet

An exhilarating game where all students get a yarn ball and attempt to hit (only) their opponent's feet. When hit, players must perform 10 to 15 repetitions of their favorite exercise (jumping jacks for example) before returning to the game. Everyone must stay in the boundaries designated before the game and varying with available space.

Grab the Flag

Everyone must tuck in their shirts and get a flag to tuck in their back pocket or in back of pants (flag belts work best if they are available). While staying inside the boundaries, children chase or dodge others, attempting to pull their flag or keep from getting theirs pulled. If pulled, a player must perform 10 to 15 repetitions of their favorite exercise (jumping jacks for example) before returning to the game. A player cannot guard their flag to prevent others from pulling it.

Cooperative Activities (P-5)

Objective

The cooperative games unit contains innovative and exciting activities designed to instill and improve initiative, problem solving, teamwork, and communication skills. The cooperative games unit should be introduced early in the school year to introduce and reinforce the character traits necessary to function in and out of physical education class.

Equipment

- Hula hoops (20-25)
- Folded gymnastics mats (3 per group)
- Bucket full of lightweight balls (1 per group)
- Plank (1), approximately two inches thick, six inches wide, and eight feet long.
- Standing targets (3 per group) (See Eight Station layout for setup.)
- Hoops (2 per group)
- Balloons (5 per group)
- Noodles (1 per person)
- Blindfolds (1 per student)
- Carpet squares, at least 18-inch square (3 per group)
- Nerf-like soccer balls (5-6)
- Scooters (2 per group)
- Traffic cones (10-12)
- Playground balls (3 per group)
- Long rope (1 per group)
- Hockey stick (1 per group)
- Yarn balls (10-15 per group)
- Any other equipment deemed necessary to increase or decrease difficulty.

Procedure

Provide a brief demonstration of each activity and proper safety. Remember, consider your class size and the equipment or space available when adding new activities or selecting ideas from the following activities. Also, know that you can easily modify any of the following activities. All activities include age-level appropriateness beside them. Use overall class comprehension of each game's objective to determine each day's progression to the next activity in the cooperatives games unit.

To start this unit off, explain or ask children what *cooperation* means and what it involves to be successful. Explain what this unit is all about and what they are expected to learn from the cooperative game activities.

Musical Madness (K-5)

Instruct students to find their own personal space within the gym. Scatter 20 or so hula hoops around the gym floor (see floor layout on page 45). Instruct the students that when the music begins, they need to move around the gym. When the music stops, though, they are to quickly get inside of a hula hoop (there may be more than one person inside a hoop). Ask them if they think that they would be able to get everyone into a hoop again if there were fewer hoops? At this point, take a couple of hoops off the floor. Start the music again and continue with this progression. Teamwork and cooperation truly play a big part in this game, especially when there are only a few hoops left! *What is the least number of hula hoops the class can get down to so that everybody is included?*

Circle the Circle (K-5)

Divide students into two or three groups. Instruct each group to form a large circle and to hold hands. Explain to them that the only rule is that they cannot let go of each other's hands. The object is for each circle to move a hula hoop from one person to another completely around the circle without letting go of any hands. Challenge each group to see how long it takes them to pass the hoop around the circle and back to the starting point. After the first time, challenge the other groups to beat the time of the winning group. If they can move one hoop with relative ease, simply add another hoop and send it the opposite direction. If a new hoop is added, it must be able to fit through the existing hoop.

Hula Hoops
Musical Madness Layout

VARIATIONS

Once each group has gotten the hang of it, combine all the groups to form one huge group. Challenge the group to create a class record to see how long it takes to get all the way around the hoop.

Thread the Needle: Now instruct students to go back to their original groups and to form a straight line. The first person in line holds a hoop perpendicular to the floor. The last person in line, followed by everyone else, must pass through the hoop, one at a time, following the same rules of Circle the Circle—that is, they all must hold hands as they pass through the hoop, and they all must see how fast they can pass through. When the last person, who is holding the hoop, passes through it, the group has "thread the needle."

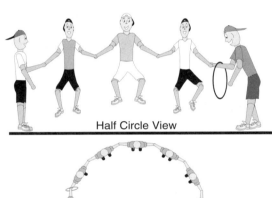

Half Circle View

Overhead View

Wizards, Elves, and Giants (2-5)

Divide the class into two equal teams, one team on each side of the gym. This activity is similar to "rock, paper, scissors." The giants beat the wizards, the wizards beat the elves, and the elves beat the giants. Demonstrate the different signs and noises each character should make. For example, if the giant is chosen, students at the signal stand tall, with arms stretched high over their heads, roaring like lions. If wizards are chosen, students stand at regular height with arms pointed forward, wiggling fingers chanting *Whooooo!* If elves are chosen, have the students squat down low, with hands on the ground, palms up, wiggling their fingers, shrieking *Eeeeeee!*

Elf   Wizard   Giant

Each round, students huddle up with their team and come up with what they think will beat the other team. Instruct students to select a second choice in case the first game is a tie—that is, in the event that two teams choose the same character. Once they have made their choices, have each team line up with their toes touching the middle line in the gym. The teacher says *"one, two, three"*, upon which all teams *clearly* act out their first chosen character. The team that wins must chase the other team. (Remember, giants beat the wizards; the wizards beat the elves; the elves beat the giants.)

If the winners tag members from the other team before they reach the "safe zone" (located past the end line on each side of the gym), then those opposing members are now on the other team. This game can go on and on because players are constantly changing sides. If players cross over the line prematurely or on accident, they must automatically join the other team.

Frogger (K-5)

Divide the class into 8 to 15 groups consisting of at least three children. Instruct these groups to form lines along the sidelines of the gym, facing the court area. Each group, if possible, has three same-colored hula hoops (lily pads). All three students from each group will be active at the same time.

The object is for one member of the group (the frog) to move across the pond without getting wet by touching the gym floor outside of the hula hoop. Two helpers (tadpoles) are to continually move the lily pads forward so that the frog has a place to jump. The two tadpoles are allowed in the water. Once the frogs make it to the other side of the gym (the pond), they must return using the same method. After each trip across the pond, each frog must switch places with one of the tadpoles. Continue this process until everyone has had a turn.

If a frog lands in the water, that frog must start over from the beginning. It is important that everyone has the chance to be both a frog and a tadpole. Remind students to place the lily pads within jumping distance, but not *too* short. This is cooperative game of speed to test how quickly they can cross the pond.

Blob Tag (K-5)

This is a traditional favorite with some slight twists. Each game begins with three children who are selected to be "It". Each It must put on one of three different color jerseys so that at the end of the game, everyone can distinguish which It made the biggest "blob."

Begin by starting the music and instructing the Its to try to tag anyone in the boundaries, except for the other Its. Once tagged, players must join hands or elbows with the It and attempt to tag someone else. When others are tagged, they too must join hands or elbows and attempt to tag someone else. This pattern continues until the entire class is a huge blob, catching everything in its path. This game encourages teamwork and communication because they are all connected to one another, attempting to move together as one blob.

Zoo Animals (K-5)

Each student is given a blindfold and privately assigned a zoo animal (e.g., lion, elephant, walrus, monkey, snake). Students are then scattered throughout the gym. On the teacher's signal, they must now find their animal groups and herd together, continually making their animal noise to reach any lost members of their group. No one may talk or peek through the blindfolds at anytime. Students can only make their proper animal noise to locate the others in their groups. Remind all blindfolded students to always walk with their hands straight out in front of them to avoid any kind of collision. Children get a kick out of this hilarious game!

Additional idea: Instruct students to partner up and decide on any one animal whose noise they would both like to make. Tell them to go to opposite sides of the gym and on the teacher's signal to turn around 5 to 10 times and begin making their animal noise. The object is for students to find their partner, amid all the other animal noises, while blindfolded. Once their partners are found, they must sit down against a side wall and quietly watch the rest of the activity. The game is extremely hilarious to watch when it gets down to the last few!

Hula Hut Relay (3-5)

Provide a quick, one-time demonstration of how to build a hula hut. To build one, place one hoop on the ground (the foundation). Place two hoops on the inside edge of the foundation, but on opposite sides of each other. Lean them together at 45-degree angles. Place two more hoops on the inside edge of the foundation, but on opposite sides of the other two hoops. Again, lean them together at 45-degree angles over the first two hoops. The sixth hoop, which is the roof, is placed on top to hold the walls in place.

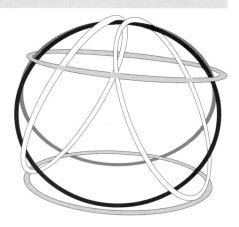

To begin, form groups of four to eight, and give each team six hula hoops. On the signal, each group works together, building their hula hut as quickly as possible. Once the hut is completed, each team must successfully get all team members through one side of the hut and out the other without knocking it down. If the hut is knocked down, they must quickly repair it and attempt again to get everyone through the hut. The first team to complete this wins! Remember that *everyone* must go through the hut. Play another round and see who can do it the fastest.

 VARIATIONS

Add difficulty by making a few students in each group wear blindfolds. Teams must now use lots of verbal communication (no touching!) to get their teammates through the hula hut.

Have the students make up their own method of getting through the huts. For fun, challenge them to build another hut on the existing hut. Hula hut building also can be a fun activity for all children on Fun Days. *How many levels can you build?*

Piranhas or Pals (2-5)

Choose three or four students to be the piranhas. They wear red jerseys and crawl around or ride on scooters. Divide the rest of the class into groups of five and give each group three carpet squares. The object of the game is to get your entire team across the Amazon River (the width or length of gym floor) without being eaten by the piranhas. Inform them that lack of teamwork results in choosing the piranhas and that teamwork results in choosing your pals.

Teams attempt to cross the Amazon River by using their three lily pads (carpet squares). Anyone landing in the river results in that team starting all over again. Piranhas are on alert for anyone landing in the river. If this occurs, they immediately report it to the teacher, who sends them back to start. Another rule: A human hand must always be in contact with a lily pad for it to stay afloat. Any piranha spotting any lily pad without someone's hand on it may take it to the teacher. That team must now achieve the task with only two lily pads. Each team that successfully gets across the Amazon is declared a team that works well together.

 VARIATION

If students are easily successful, then make one or two players from each team wear blindfolds. Try timing each round to see who can do it the quickest.

Anthills (3-5)

Scatter yarn balls or various soft objects on the gym floor. All of the various objects represent anthills. Enough anthills should be spread out so that moving through the area is challenging. Instruct students to partner up. Explain that the goal is to get from one end of the area to the other without touching any of the anthills, and the challenge is that one of the partners is blindfolded. The other partner must assist the blindfolded partner by only giving verbal instructions to direct them through the field of anthills. Remind all blindfolded students to always walk with their hands straight out in front of them to avoid any kind of collision. There can be no physical contact. All groups must start over if contact is made with an anthill. Remember, no peeking!

Silly Safari (P-5)

This activity really tests their trust and cooperation. Give everyone in the class a blindfold, then instruct him or her to partner up, and as a pair, choose one animal each member likes. Divide each team by sending one person to cone A and one to cone B, which are located on opposite ends of the gym. Students at each cone line up, then stand with their hands on the shoulders of the person in front of them. Once their blindfolds are on, explain that they are about to go on a safari, and the rule is that at no time can anyone peek. Note: This activity is best done with two teachers, where each teacher can be in charge of one group.

To begin, lead each group on a walk (the teacher is not blindfolded, of course). Walk them over, under, around, up, down, or anywhere to arouse their senses. Lead one group in the opposite direction of the other group. Make sure to give clear commands on how to walk. Tell students that they need to communicate with each other (especially to the person behind them) to inform of any obstacles that lie before them. Clear communication is essential!

Once each group has walked around for at least 10 minutes, take both groups to an open area. Then take one of the groups to another location about 30 to 40 yards away while the other group simply waits where they are. Remaining blindfolded, all students must now find their partner by making the sound of the animal they chose together (like in the game Zoo Animals).

Circle Soccer (P-5)

Divide the class into equal groups of six to eight. Instruct students to put their arms around each other to form a circle. Place a soccer ball on the ground inside of each circle. The object of the game is to get the soccer ball down the gym, around their team's cone, and back without it coming out of the circle. If the ball comes out of the circle, they immediately must stop, grab hands, and as quickly as possible, sing a song, such as "Ring Around the Rosie," the Barney "I Love You" song, or some other funny song. They must sing the song before they can start over from the beginning. Everyone must be in the circle, and everyone must participate in the song. Remember that this is all about teamwork and cooperation. The first team to make it down and back wins.

HINT

If needed during the game, inform the class that the team that goes slower while maintaining a tight group usually wins! Play until most groups are successful at least once.

Team Rally (3-5)

Team Rally definitely improves teamwork and cooperation among groups in your class. First, divide the class into groups of four to eight. The object of this game is for each group to place the gymnastics mat onto their two scooters, with one passenger and all the miscellaneous items (10 yarn balls, 3 playground balls, hula hoop, and hockey stick). Players from each team must transport their passenger and the items to the opposite end of the gym and back. If at any time a passenger or an item in transit touches the ground, the group must gather all items and return to start to begin again. Remind each group that they may transport the items and the passenger any way they choose, as long as they do not touch the floor or any of the pushers.

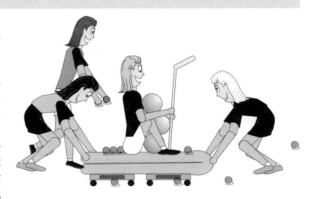

At the half-court line and at the opposite end of the gym, place a cone in each group's pathway that each group must circle. They must circle a cone one time in the center, one time at the end, and once again at the center. To win, each person in the group must be transported down and back, one time. Remind them that the pushers may only push the mat and may not touch the person or any of the equipment on the mat at any time. The first team to complete this process wins.

Don't Blow It (2-5)

Divide class into groups of four to eight students. Each team approaches a set of three standing targets. Located inside every hoop on one side of the target is one noodle per person and five balloons. Explain that each team's goal is to get all five balloons through each target and into the hoop on the other side.

Note: Stacked boxes or gymnastics mats can also be used for standing targets. Balloons would then go over the target, instead of through the target. If enough equipment is not available then add two or more cooperative games stations and have students switch stations every 5 to 10 minutes.

Before they start, remind students that it is crucial to brainstorm ideas to accomplish the task successfully. After students have played a few minutes, discuss some of the problem-solving and critical thinking techniques each team used.

Don't Blow It

⚠ Reminder

Each player may only touch one noodle. The noodle is the only thing that can be used to move the balloons. Any balloon contacting the floor or someone else results in starting the game completely over. Balloons already made into the opposite hoop must also be returned. Once an infraction is made, all players and balloons must regroup at their team's hula hoop before starting again. Noodles cannot be bent or wrapped around the balloon.

HINT

Not all noodles have to be used. A player can hold the end of a teammate's noodle and not break the rule because the rule states that "each player may only touch one noodle." Both players are still only touching one noodle.

Most students quickly react by hitting balloons by themselves, which usually results in failure. Remind students that this is a teamwork game. How can they use teamwork by getting everyone involved and still be successful? Do all the balloons have to be hit at the same time? Do the balloons even need to be hit? Can some players stand on each side of the standing targets? Encourage your students to ponder these questions before they start.

VARIATION

After a team messes up, give all groups the perception that the original group must either sit out for two to five minutes or their day is done in physical education. This really makes them sit down, brainstorm, and plan a strategy before automatically jumping right into the activity. I have never sat a group out the entire class, though, because eventually every group messes up at least once and chooses to focus more on teamwork. But once the teams think they are going to miss the rest of the class, I take the opportunity to relate the challenge to real-life challenges that they may encounter some day. To help them relate the challenge to their lives, I make up a scenario and include things such as teamwork, leadership, listening, brainstorming, and selflessness.

Reminder

There are many different solutions to this activity. Encourage the students to have fun figuring them out.

Walking the Plank (3-5)

Note: Although it will not represent the thickness of a mat, you can use carpet pieces to represent the width and length of a mat. For planks, vinyl fencing is lightweight and works the best. At least three or four of these stations need to be setup. If enough equipment is not available or if there are too many students, then combine this activity with two or more cooperative games stations and have students switch stations every 5 to 10 minutes.

Divide the class into teams of 8 to 16. Each team goes to a set of three gymnastic mats (the life rafts), strategically placed by the teacher. Located at each area is one plank and one bucket full of balls (food supply and medical kit). Explain that each team's goal is to get everyone from the first life raft to the second life raft and finally to the third life raft without touching the shark-infested waters. Remind students before they start that brainstorming ideas to accomplish the task is crucial to be successful. After students have played a few minutes, discuss some of the problem-solving and critical thinking techniques each team used.

Reminder

Only three people are allowed on a life raft at any time. Players, planks, food supply, and medical kit buckets may not touch the water. If this occurs, the team must start completely over from the beginning. Only one person may be on the plank. People waiting to enter the first life raft and those exiting the third life raft are the only ones allowed to be on the ground. Players may not physically assist their team once they step off the third life raft. Only one person is allowed to touch the medical kit at any time! The first person to touch it is the only person who is allowed to touch it the remainder of the game. Also, this one person may never carry the food supply and medical kit bucket across the water.

HINT

Push the bucket across the plank, or place the bucket handle on the plank and slide it across. Make sure that it does not touch the water or that nobody else touches it on the other side. See if they can figure this one out on their own.

VARIATION

If a team messes up then give all groups the perception that their day is done in physical education or they must sit out for two to five minutes. This will really make them sit down, brainstorm, and plan a strategy before automatically jumping right into the activity. I have never sat a group out the entire class though, because eventually all groups mess up at least once. Instead, once all teams think they are going to miss the rest of the class, I take the opportunity to relate the challenge to a real-life challenges they may encounter some day. I include things such as teamwork, leadership, listening, brainstorming, and selflessness in the scenario I make up to help them relate the game challenge to their lives.

Reminder

There are many different solutions to this activity. Encourage your students to have fun figuring them out. If a team is successful, challenge them to make it back to where they started.

Survivors (3-5)

The scenario is that a huge volcano has erupted, and all of the inhabitants of the island must evacuate to survive. The object of this activity is for everyone in each group (six to eight students per group) to cross the molten lava river with their boats (scooter boards) along with their 15 to 20 medicine and food containers (yarn balls) to the safe yet desolate island (the other side of the gym). This game is a critical thinking exercise where each group must take their time and figure out the solution. Provide only these rules and instructions. (1) Anyone touching the lava dies, and the group must start over. (2) There are three safe rock formations to stand on (hula hoops already set out for each group). These rock formations remain stationary. (3) Each team can use the equipment to help cross the lava river. The equipment can touch the lava. (4) All medicine must be transported to the safe island. Because it is so valuable and delicate, it can't be thrown, dropped, or carried by just one person. If any of the medicine or food touches the lava, the group must completely start over from the beginning. (5) The group has to completely start over each time anyone touches the lava, a boat gets stuck in the middle, or they drop a medicine or food container—even if they have someone on the safe island. (6) No one may run and jump to a rock formation!

The following solutions involve games of five to eight players per team:

■ Student A gets the long rope and jumps on a boat. Using the oar (hockey stick), the student moves across the lava to the first rock formation. Student A gets off the boat onto the rock and ties the rope to the boat. While holding onto the rope, the child slides the boat and oar back to the group.

The next person, student B, then moves across the lava with the assistance of the first person, who pulls the rope a little to get student B to the second rock formation. Once on the rock, student B slides everything back to the first rock. The next person, student C, then moves across the lava with the assistance of the student A, who helps pull the rope a little to get student C to the third rock formation. Once on the rock, student C slides everything back to the second rock; student B slides everything on to the first rock, then finally to the start. The next person, student D, moves across the lava with the assistance of each person on each rock, who helps pull the rope to get student D to the safe island. Student D has to get to the island before repeating the process to get the boat back.

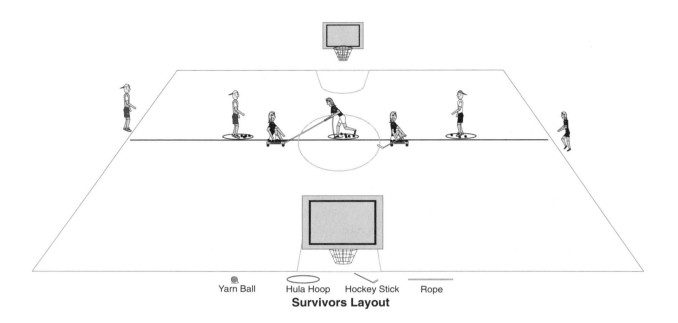

Yarn Ball   Hula Hoop   Hockey Stick   Rope
Survivors Layout

At this point, one person at the start loads up all of the medicine onto the boat. Student A (at the first rock) pulls the boat toward the rock, then passes the rope to student B (at the second rock) who pulls it to student C and so on, until it reaches the person on the safe island. With the medicine secure, the rope and boat return to rock one, where people are ready to travel across to the safe island. The remaining students travel with the assistance of those on the rocks until everyone can be pulled or can row to safety.

■ Student A gets on a boat and takes the oar to the first rock. Student B ties the rope to the second boat and throws the other end of the rope to student A, who slowly pulls the second person to the first rock. Two people are on the first rock, and they now push the boats and rope back to the rest of the team.

Next, the remaining students turn one of the boats over (so the wheels are face up), and they place the medicine inside of it. They make sure the rope is tied to one of the handles, and they throw the other end to the people on the first rock. The two people on the first rock now pull the boat to them. Once they get the boat, they then need to unload the medicine onto the rock.

One person from the first rock must now get on the boat and use the oar to get to the second rock. There is now one person on the first rock with the medicine, and one person on the second rock. The person on the second rock must push the boat and oar back to the one on the first rock, who then pushes the scooter with the rope to the team members waiting in line.

The next person in line, student C, gets on the boat and throws one end of the rope to the person on the first rock. Again, make sure one end is tied to the boat. The person on the first rock pulls this person onto the first rock. They then push the oar and rope to the next person in line, and student D gets on the boat. The people on the first rock pull student D past them and toss the rope to the person on the second rock, who pulls student D onto the second rock.

There are now two people on both rocks. One person on the second rock turns over a boat and loads the medicine onto it. While this is happening, the other person on the second rock is using one boat and the oar to get to the third rock. When the person gets to the third rock, the person on the second rock tosses one end of the rope to the person on the third rock, who then pulls the medicine. Once the medicine gets to the third rock, it is left on the boat. The other boat and oar are passed to the second rock, where someone uses it to get to the island. Once on the island, the person on the third rock tosses the rope to the person on the island, who pulls the medicine to safety. The boat and oar are finally passed from rock to rock to get the rest to the team to safety.

Superstars and Record Breakers (3-5)

Objective

To perform a variety of challenging health and skill-related fitness components: muscular strength, muscular endurance, cardiovascular endurance, coordination, speed, agility, power, balance, and reaction time. To distinguish and understand their differences and to compete for school physical education records. All new records will be posted on the gym wall for students to see. On Fun Days, students may challenge one existing record. When the teacher is ready, students may attempt to break the record of their choice. Some records allow for up to three attempts; see the records below for clarification.

Equipment

- Wall-mounted pegboard (1)
- Plastic cups (6)
- Short ropes (10-12)
- Pennies in a cup (30-50)
- Pogo sticks (3-6)
- Basketballs (2-4)
- Hula hoops (6-8)
- Vertical jump lines (measured on the wall using both inches and centimeters).
- Broad jump lines (measured on floor)
- Wooden boxes (2 or 3) (24" by 24" by 10")
- Gymnastics mats (2 or 3) (Alternative for wooden boxes. A folded gymnastics mat is approximately 10 to 12 inches high and 24 inches wide.)
- Traffic cones (to section off each station)

Procedure

Set aside one week to introduce health- and skill-related fitness components, and have students practice the skills to establish your school's physical education records. Students have many opportunities to practice each skill by rotating counterclockwise every two to four minutes to each station. During this week, each class period establishes unofficial records. At the end of the week, the best record for each skill is recorded for future Fun Day challenges. Only on future Fun Days can students challenge an existing record.

Broadcast the latest record set and who broke it during the morning announcements. A message board mounted in the gym or bulletin board can also display all records and the students who set them. Update the records as soon as one has been broken. To denote the skills that allow individual records for both a boy and girl, a "B/G" is placed by the station.

Records to Be Set and Broken:

- Pogo Stick Jumps (balance and agility): How many consecutive jumps?
- Foul Shots (coordination): How many made in one minute?
- Elbow-Penny Catch (coordination and reaction time): Total number of pennies that can be caught. Stacking them on your elbow, then swing hand downward to catch them. Whatever amount is attempted must be caught for it to count. In other words, if 10 are attempted and only 9 are caught, the attempt does not count for either 10 or 9.
- Consecutive Push-Ups (B/G) (muscular strength): Must start in the up-position; chest must touch cup.
- Consecutive Partner Sit-Ups (B/G) (muscular strength and endurance): Partners must hand a beanbag to their partner between each sit-up. One sit-up by each student counts

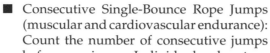

as one; a dropped or thrown bean bag, elbows touching the ground, or incomplete sit-ups do not count. Continue counting all sit-ups until a major pause occurs.

■ Consecutive Single-Bounce Rope Jumps (muscular and cardiovascular endurance): Count the number of consecutive jumps before messing up. Individual and partner records can be established.

■ Peg Board Challenge (B/G) (muscular strength, muscular endurance, and coordination): The 13-hole Peg-Board is hung on the gym wall. Students climb up the Peg-Board, and each time a peg is removed and placed into a new hole, they receive a point. The most points scored before letting go holds the new record.

■ Consecutive Foul Shots (coordination): *How many shots can you make in a row?*

■ Vertical Jump and Standing Broad Jump (B/G) (power): Each student gets three attempts.

■ Hula Hoop Around Waist and Neck (coordination): *How long can you hula hoop around your waist or neck?*

■ One-Minute Jump Rope Challenge (speed and coordination): Students can establish both individual and partner records for total number of jumps in one minute.

■ One-Minute Box/Mat Jump Challenge (speed, coordination, and agility): To begin, stand at the side of the mat, and start the clock on the student's first move to land on top of the mat. The student must jump on top of the mat, then off the mat to the other side, back to the top, and so on until one minute is up. *How many box/mat jumps can you do in a minute?* A point is awarded each time a student lands on top of the mat. Landing on the floor beside the mat does not count as a point.

■ Consecutive Box/Mat Jump Challenge (muscular strength, muscular and cardiovascular endurance, and coordination): This one isn't timed. The record is established by how many jumps a student can perform without stopping. *How many box jumps can you do in a row?*

■ Consecutive Soccer Juggles (coordination): Students juggle a soccer ball following the rules of soccer—that is, they cannot use their hands. *How many times can you soccer juggle before it hits the ground?*

■ Any other fun and goofy record that you come up with.

Noodles Skills (P-2)

Objective

To explore the various ways to manipulate a foam noodle.

Equipment

■ Noodles, 4 to 5 feet (1 per student)
■ Music

Procedure

Students get one noodle and find a seat in personal space. Explain that before anyone plays a noodle game, everyone needs to explore ways to manipulate and play with the foam noodle. Remind students at this time that hitting others with the noodles will result in the noodles being taken away!

Individual Activities

- Get a noodle and sit down in personal space to prepare for noodle activities.
- Lay your noodle on the floor. How fast can you run around your noodle? See how many times you can run around the noodle in 60 seconds. Now imitate a skier by jumping over the noodle from side to side, with feet together. How many ski jumps can you make in 60 seconds?
- On the word "go," drop your noodle to the floor and run and jump over as many noodles as you can before I say, "freeze." Now pick up a noodle and skip around the room until everyone has a noodle.
- Balance the noodle lengthwise in the palm of your hand. Move around the room while balancing it. Can you balance the noodle on the back of your hand?
- Can you balance the noodle in one hand, then pop it in the air and catch it with the other hand?
- Can you balance the noodle with any other part of your body?
- Pretend you are in a battle against an imaginary enemy. How would you defend yourself?
- Can you twirl the noodle like a baton? Now pretend you are a helicopter.
- Toss your noodle up in the air, and see if you can catch it before it hits the ground. If you drop it, you must do five jumping jacks before continuing.
- How high can you toss your noodle and still catch it? Shoot the noodle up like a missile. Can you hit the ceiling? Now gather in the center. Count down from five, and shoot your missiles up toward the sky as high as possible.
- Now pretend you are in the Olympics. Throw your noodle like a javelin. How far can you throw it?
- Who can toss the noodle in the air, touch the floor, and then catch it?
- How many times can you clap before catching your noodle?
- Can you toss your noodle up, spin around and then catch it?
- Create a new way to play with your foam noodle.
- Free time—practice previously learned skills with the noodle.

Partner Activities

- Toss and catch the noodle with a partner. Now toss and catch both noodles.
- How high can you toss the noodle to your partner and still have them catch it?
- How far away can you get and still be able to toss the noodle to your partner so they can catch it?
- Toss the noodle to your partner while they are moving. Can they catch it?

■ Can you throw your noodle through a hula hoop held by your partner? Now try throwing your noodle through the hoop after your partner rolls it. Try spinning the hoop, and see if your partner can throw the noodle through it.

■ How far back can you move and still make the noodle through the hoop?

■ Volley a balloon back and forth to your partner with your noodles without allowing the balloon to hit the floor.

■ Now sandwich the noodle sideways in between yourselves. Move around the room without dropping the noodle.

■ Now let's play a game. With the noodle still in between both of you, can you steal another team's noodle by ripping it out from between them? Remember, each time you get your noodle ripped out, you have to go outside the boundaries and do 10 jumping jacks before reentering the game.

■ Can you and some friends draw a picture, make a letter of the alphabet, or spell a word on the ground with your group's combined noodles?

■ Free time—practice previously learned skills with the noodle.

■ Balloon Blitz

■ Outbreak

■ Noodle Hockey Mania

Scooter Hockey Skills (P-2)

Objective

To develop and learn the hockey skills of passing and receiving, dribbling and shooting. To enhance teamwork and cooperation with others while participating on scooter boards at various stations.

Equipment

■ Traffic cones to section off each station

■ Poly spots (30-40)

■ Hockey balls (15-20)

■ Scooters (25-40)

■ Short-handled hockey sticks (20-30) (Replacement blades sold in most physical education catalogs work best.)

■ Hockey goals (3-4)

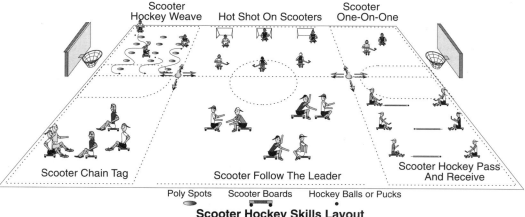

Scooter Hockey Skills Layout

56

- Colored jersey (1)
- Blindfolds (1 per pair of students)

Procedure

The teacher demonstrates each activity station (rules and how to play). Children are then divided into equal groups to play at the following stations. From the list, choose which stations will work best for you. Add or eliminate per available scooters and class size.

Rules and Safety

- Children must always sit on the scooter boards.
- Absolutely no high sticking!
- Remind all students that the first whistle means to get ready to rotate, which means cleaning the station for the next group. The second whistle means to rotate.

Games and Activities

- Scooter Chain Tag: Each child gets on a scooter with one being "It" (this child puts on the colored jersey). Everyone else tries to avoid the It, but must stay inside the coned-off area. Tagged players must connect on with the It by grabbing each other's scooter handles or by locking arms. Once connected to the chain, players can't let go and must use teamwork to move around. Continue this process until there is a complete chain. Start over with the last person getting tagged being the It.
- Scooter Follow the Leader: Students partner up and sit on a scooter with only one partner putting on a blindfold. The partner without the blindfold gives simple verbal cues so that the blindfolded partner can follow while moving around within the boundaries. Make it clear that the person without the blindfold is responsible for the safety of the blindfolded partner. Make sure students switch roles at least once within the time limit.
- Scooter Hockey Pass and Receive: Each child has a scooter and a short-handled hockey stick. While sitting on their scooters, children control the ball with their stick before passing and receiving the ball. The teacher needs to decide whether children may move around to practice these skills or perform these skills from designated spots.
- Scooter One-on-One: Students partner up, and each child gets a scooter and a short-handled hockey stick. One partner gets control of the ball first, manipulating it with the hockey stick blade while playing "Keep Away" from their partner. Partners try to steal the ball and resume control of it. Continue playing to see who can maintain control of the ball the longest.

! Reminder

Using some form of border patrol is great to keep students from chasing balls all over the gym. Remember to stay inside the coned-off area.

- Scooter Hot Shot: Children practice dribbling and shooting at a goal while moving on their scooter. For more fun and participation, use a goalie (with or without a scooter).
- Scooter Hockey Weave: While dribbling and controlling a hockey ball with their stick, children weave on scooters in and out of the poly spots, spread out in rows of six to eight.

Scooter Skills Galore (P-5)

Objective

To explore the many exciting ways to manipulate and control scooter boards while participating both independently and with a partner.

Equipment

- Traffic cones (20-24)
- Scooters (20-24) (preferably 3-6 different color variations)
- A variety of colored construction paper or colored juggling rings (the rings fit perfectly over traffic cones)

Procedure

First, set up cones approximately three yards apart (10 to 12 on each side of the gym). In front of each cone on one side of the gym, place two same-colored scooters. Directly across from each cone on the other side of the gym, place another cone with a specific color of construction paper taped on it or a juggling ring that matches the color scooter directly across from it. For example, if one team is red, they can only send two members at a time (two same-colored scooters), and they can only go around the cone directly across from them with either red construction paper or a red juggling ring on it. Each group of four to six performs the scooter activities in a relay fashion; all children take turns by going down and around their own cone and back. When children return, they must hand their scooter to the next person in line.

Before anyone uses the scooters, though, the teacher or student volunteers need to demonstrate each scooter skill (rules and how to drive). Explain that all students have earned a scooter driver's license. If there is *any* reckless driving, their license can be revoked by the police (teachers). Relate actual driving experiences, such as what could happen if you drive in the wrong lane, drive recklessly, or drink and drive. And one last rule: Because students have to wait their turn before scooting, anyone not on a scooter must dance. Dance contests or some form of exercise challenge works great and keeps everyone moving.

Cover scooter skills in the following list. Choose the ones that work best for you, adding or eliminating any to complement class size and available equipment. Remember, two students from each group scoot at a time, but feel free to add an additional scooter to any group if you deem it safe.

Rules and Safety

- Scooters are *not* to be used as skateboards or missiles (sliding across floor with hands and feet off the ground).
- Watch fingers, and hold grips at all times. Do not drag hands under scooter.
- Never let go of a scooter board, with or without a passenger.
- Driver's licenses will be taken (child will briefly lose their scooter) for not looking where they're going, crashing, sliding, or careless driving!
- Because each group has two people going at a time, remind them to take extra care not to crash into teammates.

Single Scooter Tasks

The following tasks require only one scooter per team.

- Seated Relay (forward/backward): Have students sit upright on scooter, always gripping handles or sides. They propel themselves by pushing with their feet.
- Hamster Crawl: Students place knees on scooter and lean forward. Using their hands, they propel themselves forward (pulling) or backward (pushing). Remind students to place hands out to the side to avoid the wheels.

- Alligator Crawl: Tell students to lie face down with the scooter under the middle of their body. They should push with their feet and pull with their hands, like an alligator crawling on the ground.

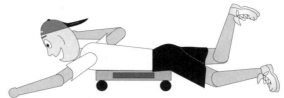

- Pretzel Style: Students sit cross-legged on a scooter. They propel themselves with their hands out to the side or by leaning back onto their hands and pushing. Go forward or backward.

- Crab Walk: Students sit on the floor and place their feet on top of the scooter in front of them. They lift their bodies off the floor with their hands, and crab walk forward or backward. This one is strenuous!

- Bear Crawl: Students grip the handles or sides of the scooter while running behind the scooter. Look out for this one. If they're going too fast and fall to their knees, it is easy for them to get carpet burns. Because of the speed of this skill, allow only one scooter to go at a time.

- Backin' Up: Have students lie on the scooter face up, with the middle portion of their back on the scooter. Students clasp hands behind their neck to protect their head. Everything is upside-down, so drive slowly while pushing with their feet.

- Kick Start: The student centers one knee on the scooter. With the other leg out to the side, they propel themselves forward with their foot, kind of like kick starting a motorcycle.

- Walrus Walk: Students get into push-up position, and place shins and feet on top of the scooter. Next they move forward, dragging their scooter behind them. This one definitely works the upper body!

Partner Scooter Tasks

The following tasks require partners and two scooters per pair.

- Siamese Twins: All children sit on their scooter next to their partner. Have them grab their partner's closest handle; each partner should be holding a handle. Each group must use teamwork and cooperation to successfully stay together.

■ Back-to-Back: Each child, while sitting on the scooter, gets back-to-back with the partner and grabs the partner's scooter handles. Each group must then cooperate by ensuring that the person going forward *pulls* with feet and the person going backward *pushes* with feet. Then switch roles.

■ Face-to-Face: All children, while sitting on their scooter, face their partner and place their feet in each other's lap. They then propel themselves forward or backward, using only their hands.

■ Ambulance: One child lies facing up on both scooters. The partner grabs the feet and pulls the "ambulance" down around the cone and back. Then switch roles.

■ Train: The students sit on their scooters, facing forward, one partner behind the other. The engines are the people in front who pull with their legs; the cabooses are the people in back who lean back and push with their hands with their feet wrapped around their partner's waist. Have them switch roles.

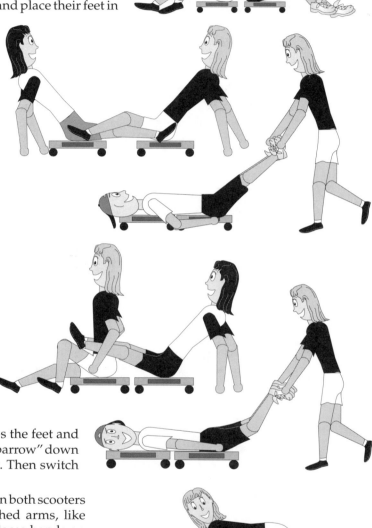

■ Wheelbarrow: One child lies face down on both scooters. The partner grabs the feet and pulls or pushes the "wheelbarrow" down around the cone and back. Then switch roles.

■ Superman: One child lies on both scooters face down with outstretched arms, like Superman. The partner places hands on the back and pushes Superman, who helps steer around the cone with the outstretched arms. Then switch roles.

■ Monster Truck: One child places knees on the back scooter and leans forward to place hands on the front scooter. The partner pushes the "monster truck" by placing hands on the partner's back. Then switch roles.

■ Dragster with Frisbee: One child sits on the back scooter with feet on top of the scooter in front. The partner places hands on the back and pushes while the driver pretends to steer with the Frisbee. Then they switch roles.

■ Horse and Buggy: Same as the Dragster, but this time the partner who pulls has a jump rope around the waist (like horse reins). The other partner holds the ends of the reins. Have them switch roles.

The following bonus skills should only be attempted if the class has had no problems following the previous scooter safety rules.

■ The Spinner: One child lies face up on both scooters. The partner grabs the feet and turns the "spinner" in circles while going down and back. To protect their heads, have them clasp their hands behind their necks. Then switch roles.

■ Pile-Up Relay: Both partners lie on both scooters face down with one partner on top (like a double Superman). Use hands or whatever it takes to get down and back!

Games and Activities

■ Scoot 'n' Shoot
■ Team Trashball
■ Scooter Scavenger
■ Treasure Quest
■ Sonic Boom

Scooter Chain Tag

Each child gets on a scooter with one being "It" (this child puts on the colored jersey). Everyone else tries to avoid the It, but must stay inside the coned-off area. If tagged, a player must connect with the It by grabbing scooter handles or locking arms. Once connected to the chain, players can't let go and must use teamwork to move around. Continue this process until there is a complete chain. Start over with the last person getting tagged being the It.

Striking and Kicking Activities

This section provides lead-up activities for games that involve striking and kicking. They should be taught before implementing any supporting games or formal sports. These basic skills will give students more confidence when they begin playing more highly organized activities.

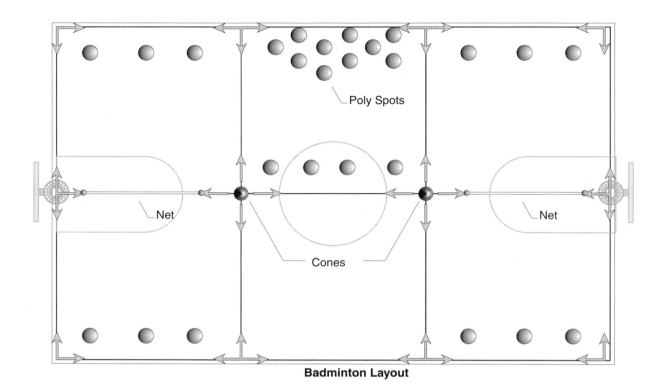

Badminton Layout

Badminton (3-5)

Objective

To introduce and improve the skills necessary to play badminton. A teacher- or student-led demonstration will be given before class to help students learn how to grip a racket and hit a birdie, how to volley with a partner, how to hit a birdie into or at a target, and how to serve over a net. See Badminton layout on page 62 for setup.

Equipment

- Standards with nets (2) (badminton or volleyball nets will do)
- Badminton rackets and birdies (20-30) (Short and long-handled foam rackets are wonderful for children having a hard time hitting the birdies with the badminton racket.)
- Hula hoops (15-20) (to be used as targets on the wall and floor)
- Poly spots (30) (to designate where to stand)
- Traffic cones (to section off each station)

Procedure

Divide classes into three groups and rotate them every 10 to 15 minutes so that each group has an opportunity to participate at each of the three stations. Explain and demonstrate what to do at each station. Set up stations one and three on opposite ends of the gym. Set up a net at stations one and three along with enough poly spots, rackets and birdies for each of the participants. At stations one and three place four poly spots on each side of the net with a racket on top of them. On one side of the net, place a birdie on each spot. Instruct students to serve to their partner directly across from them on the other side of the net.

Set up station two between stations one and three. Randomly spread hoops around the station. Place them close to a wall for a barrier. Place poly spots approximately 10 to 20 yards away from the hoops with one racket and three to five birdies on each spot. This station should be set up so that birdies cannot be hit into stations one and three.

62

Because of space and class size limitations, focus on badminton skills, rather than on rules of play. Do this for the sole purpose of maximizing participation.

Skills to reinforce during the demonstrations at stations one and three:

1. How to grip racket and where to hold it.
2. How to hold and drop birdie.
3. Arm is always slightly bent, never stiff—use wrist.
4. Underhand serve with follow-through of arm.
5. Practice service and volley over the net with your partner.

Skill to reinforce during the demonstration at station two: How to aim and hit a birdie at various targets and various distances.

Rules and Safety

■ In some areas, especially with a large class, children must look around before swinging the rackets.

■ Children must put equipment in its proper place before teacher allows rotation.

■ If they are available, children should have the option to use short-handled foam paddles instead of the long-handled badminton rackets.

VARIATION

If class sizes are small, teach regulation badminton rules and play. Designate one station for playing two-on-two badminton.

Balloon and Paddle Skills (P-2)

Objective

To develop and enhance visual tracking skills, hand-eye coordination, and teamwork through the use of balloons and paddles.

Equipment

■ Balloons (20) (plus a few extra when some pop)

■ Short- and long-handled foam paddles (32)

■ Tennis balls, scooters, yarn balls, and beaded ropes (8 each)

■ Gatorskin ball (1)

■ Traffic cones (to section off each station)

Procedure

Demonstrate each activity station (rules and how to play). Divide children into equal groups to play at the following stations. Choose the ones that you feel work best with your class objective and class equipment.

Games and Activities

■ Balloon Volley (with a paddle): Challenge children to keep their balloon from touching the floor by using their foam paddles. *How many times can you hit it before it hits the ground?*

■ Balancing Act: Challenge children to balance their yarn ball on their paddle as long as they can. Balance it at different levels. Make up ways to balance the yarn ball.

■ Balloon Foot Volley: Children sit on the floor (or get in the crab-walk position) and try to keep the balloon from touching the ground. The key is that children can only use their feet.

- Balloon Volley: Challenge children to keep their balloon from touching the floor by using any body part. *How many times can you hit it before it hits the ground?*

- Paddle Balloon Volley (with a partner): Challenge partners to keep their balloon from touching the floor by using their foam paddles. *How many times can you hit it before it hits the ground?*

- Paddle Serve to Buckets: Children form four to six lines. Using short or long-handled foam paddles, they take turns making underhand serves, attempting to make the birdies go into the buckets.

- Balloon Keep It Up: Challenge children to work together and try to keep all balloons (two or three) from touching the floor by using any body part. *How many times can your team hit them before they touch the ground?*

- Paddle Dribble: Challenge children to dribble a tennis ball with their foam paddle. Dribble it at different levels, fast or slow, and so on.

- Balloon Blitz

Hockey and Game Skills (3-5)

Objective

To develop, improve, and demonstrate the various skills of passing and receiving a hockey ball, playing one-on-one, weave dribbling, shooting a goal past a goalie, and performing in game-type situations of hockey. Scooter Marco Polo and Grab the Flag were selected as additional stations to maximize participation.

Equipment

- Poly spots (30-40)
- Hockey goals (3 or 4)

- Hockey sticks (30-35)
- Box hockey games (3 or 4)
- Hockey balls or pucks (18-20)
- Blindfolds (3-5)
- Scooter boards (8-10)
- Traffic cones or border patrol (to section off each station)

Procedure

Demonstrate each activity station (rules and how to play), then divide students into equal groups to play at the following stations. Choose only the ones that you feel work the best with your class objective and available equipment.

Rules and Safety

- No high sticking!
- Stay in designated area until signal is given to rotate.
- Always clean up on first whistle or signal.
- Rotate counterclockwise.

Games and Activities

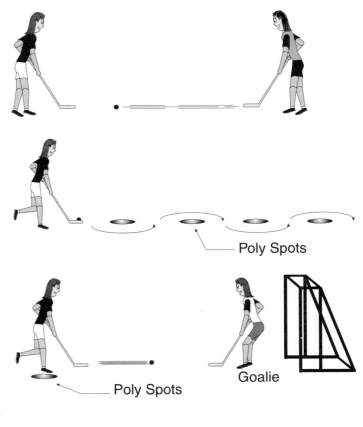

- Hockey Pass and Receive: Students pair up and stand on poly spots across from each other. Each group takes turns receiving, controlling, then passing the ball to their partner using their hockey sticks. Remember, no high sticking! Students should never raise the stick above their knee.

- Weave Dribble: Students form four to six lines and weave in and out of the poly spots, (spread out in rows of six to eight), while manipulating the ball with their hockey stick. *How fast can you go while maintaining control of the ball?*

Poly Spots

- Hockey Shot on Goal: Students form three or four lines at the poly spots. The first person from each line gets to be the goalie. The next person in line hockey dribbles the ball close to the goal and attempts to score against the goalie. Remember, no high sticking! Score or not, the player now takes the goalie's spot, and the former goalie goes to end of line.

Goalie

Poly Spots

- Hockey Mania

Hockey One-on-One

Students partner up, each getting a hockey stick. One partner gets control of the ball first by manipulating it with the hockey stick blade while playing "Keep Away" from the opposing partner, who tries to steal the ball and resume control of it. Continue playing to see who can maintain control of the ball the longest. Use some form of border patrol or barrier on the floor to keep the ball within the station boundaries. (Border patrol is used to block openings or provide enclosed wall boundaries.)

Box Hockey

This piece of equipment can either be purchased out of a physical education equipment catalog or can be made out of vinyl siding. (See physical education catalogs under Hyper Hockey for an example.) Two or three box hockey sets are ideal.

 VARIATION

Take away two side stations to play a six-on-six hockey game.

Striking Skills and Hand-Eye Coordination (P-2)

Objective

To enhance hand-eye coordination and demonstrate an understanding of striking skills through the use of hands, paddles, hockey sticks, or plastic bats.

Equipment

- Hockey pucks or balls (10-20)
- Long and short foam paddles (15-20)
- Birdies (20-30)
- Yarn balls and hula hoops (10-15)
- Plastic bats and batting tees (4-6)
- Balloons (10)
- Hockey sticks (4-6)
- Short-handled hockey sticks (6-8)
- Poly spots (43-52) (to make four hockey weave-dribbling stations and bases to show where children stand)
- Traffic cones (to section off each station)

Procedure

The teacher demonstrates each activity station (rules and how to play). Children are then divided into equal groups to play at the following stations. Select those that you feel work best for your class environment with the equipment that is readily available. See Striking Skills and Hand-Eye Coordination layout on page 67 for setup.

Note: Demonstrate the following skills: how to grip a paddle and serve, how to grip a bat and swing, how to aim and serve a birdie at objects on wall or floor, how to grip a hockey stick, how to weave dribble, and how to shoot at a goal.

Rules and Safety

- Stay in designated area, within lines where necessary.
- Always look before swinging a paddle or bat.
- A teacher will be stationed at the batting station.

Games and Activities

- Paddle Balloon Volley (to self or a partner): Challenge partners to keep their balloon from hitting the floor by using their foam paddles.
- Yarn Ball Throw to Bucket: Have the children form four to six lines with four yarn balls at each. Challenge children to throw overhand at the buckets to see how many points they can score.
- Hockey Pass and Receive: Children partner up and sit across from each other. From a seated position or on their knees, children pass a puck/ball back and forth to each other using a short-handled hockey stick.
- Hockey Weave Dribble: Children get into one of four lines and take turns weaving in and out of the poly spots, using a regular hockey stick to control the ball.
- Hitting Off a Batting Tee: Children form four to six lines five yards behind each batting tee. One child only is allowed to hit at each tee. All other children must briefly wait in line until the batter has hit each of three yarn balls provided. Each child gets to take three turns hitting the yarn ball off the tee. When a child's turn is over, he or she must carry the bat to the next child in line.
- Yarn Ball Throws at a Wall Target: Children form four to six lines with four yarn balls at each. Challenge children to throw overhand at the hula hoop targets or pictures on the wall.
- Badminton Service Into Hoops (on the ground, on the wall, or both): Children form four to six lines and perform underhand serves attempting to serve the birdies into the buckets, using short- or long-handled foam paddles.
- Serving Birdies Over a Net: Each child partners up and sits across the net from the other child. Each child then takes turns performing underhand serves over the net by hitting the birdies with short or long-handled foam paddles. The partner then serves it back.

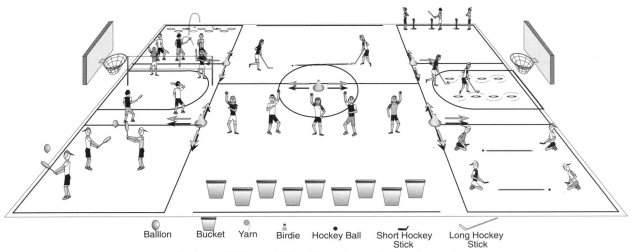

Striking Skills and Hand-Eye Coordination Layout

■ Balance and Striking Challenge: Students get behind one of four to six cones. Beside each cone is a hula hoop with a variety of types and sizes of balls. Challenge students to keep whatever object they choose balanced on their foam paddle while they go down and around their cone and back. When the objects fall off, instruct them to quickly pick it up and start from the point it was dropped. *Can you balance all of the different objects without them falling off? Which objects are the easiest and hardest to balance? Why? Can you balance more than one object at a time?*

■ Balloon Blitz

Volleyball and Hockey Skills (P-5)

Objective

To introduce and develop the individual sport skills of volleyball and hockey.

Equipment

■ Soft-spike volleyballs (12)
■ Game standards (4) with nets (2)
■ Beach balls (4-6)
■ Hockey sticks (18)
■ Z-balls or hockey pucks (10)
■ Poly spots (40-50) (or bases to indicate where students stand)
■ Traffic cones (to section off each station)

Procedure

The teacher demonstrates each activity station (rules and how to play). Divide children into equal groups to play at the following stations. Choose from the following list stations that work best for you—add or eliminate stations depending on class size or equipment available.

Games and Activities

■ Hockey Pass and Receive: Students pair up and stand on poly spots across from each other. Each pair takes turns passing the ball to each other using their hockey sticks.

 VARIATION

One-on-one hockey or hockey shot on goal.

 Reminder

Remember, no high sticking! Students should never raise the stick above the knee.

■ Partner Volleyball Bump: Students pair up and stand on poly spots across from each other. Each pair takes turns passing the ball to each other using an underhand, rainbow-like throw while the other person bumps the ball back to their partner (hands together, with thumbs and fingers pointed down, arms straight, elbows locked and forearms flat). Perform three bumps, then switch.

■ Keep It Up: Challenge children to work together by keeping the beach ball from touching the floor every time it goes over the net by using any body part but the feet. (Add one more to make it real interesting.) *How many times can your team hit it over the net before it touches the ground?*

- Underhand Serve to Target on Wall: Place hula hoops or a tape line on the wall to represent approximately where the top of the volleyball net would be. Challenge students to see how many times they can successfully serve the ball over the net. Form four to six lines; one volleyball for each line.
- Hockey Weave Dribble: Students form four to six lines and weave in and out of the poly spots while manipulating their hockey stick to control the ball.
- Hockey Mania
- Switch and Vicious Volleyball

Beach Ball Hot Potato

Challenge children to work together to keep the beach ball from touching the floor (add one more ball to make it real interesting). Every time the ball goes over the net, instruct children to catch it and immediately throw it back over like a hot potato. How many times can your team get it over the net? If the ball touches the ground, the children should quickly pick it up and get rid of it.

Chapter 2
Supporting Games and Activities

The following chapter contains innovative games and activities that are designed to provide mass-participation activities for physical education classes involving 50 to 75 elementary children. Although a majority of the games are new, you may notice that some of the games are variations of traditional favorites, enhanced with exciting new twists and names. With this in mind, consider the following tips when reading this chapter to help maximize your games and meet your program's needs:

■ I highly recommend that you tie some games in this chapter to particular lessons or that you end a unit with a particular game. For example, the Hockey Skills Unit wouldn't be complete without playing Hockey Mania, Scooter Skills Galore, Dr. Feelgood, or Scooter Scavenger.

■ Combine games that are not associated with any unit plan into a games unit, or as an alternative, make them into individual lessons.

■ Grade-level appropriateness is provided to inform which games and activities, without any modifications, work best with these age groups.

■ To adjust for your program's needs, you can modify the P-2 games and activities for the third, fourth, and fifth grades. For smaller classes, simply modify equipment, spatial, or station needs.

■ Along with your individual units, you can use and reuse these games in an endless number of combinations.

To help facilitate and ensure overall success, please remember the necessary time management components: systems for equipment setup and dispersion, signals for starting and stopping class, and methods for dealing with behavior problems.

Hot Off the Press

The first group of games in this section are new. Your students have not played them before, and they will enjoy the creativity.

Balloon Blitz (P-5)

Objective

To improve hand-eye coordination and cardiovascular fitness. This game also encourages teamwork and strategy.

Equipment

- ■ Foam noodles, four to five feet in length (1 per person) (Ideally, each team should have like-colored noodles. If like-colored noodles are not possible, then like-colored jerseys for each team works just as easily.)
- ■ Large, inflated balloons (25-50 per game) (It wouldn't hurt to have some spares just in case a balloon really gets blitzed. The more the better!)
- ■ Trashcans, barrels, boxes, or containers (2) (to hold balloons that have been scored)
- ■ Two sets of different colored jerseys (2 jerseys per set) (to designate each team's goalies)
- ■ Traffic cones (20-30) (Place these on the end lines to separate the goalies from the play area. They are not necessary, but they are helpful in preventing anyone the chance to cross the end line.)

Procedure

The object of this game is for each team to vigorously and exhaustively attempt to score the most points by hitting balloons with foam noodles to their goalies. Divide teams in half and direct each team to one side of the gym to get a noodle (and jersey, if necessary). See Balloon Blitz Layout for boundaries and setup.

From each team select two goalies to stand in their team's end zone. Place all balloons into the center circle of the gym. When you give the signal to begin, the children begin to hit every balloon to their goalies, which are standing behind them inside their team's end zone. Because goalies are not allowed to cross over the end line, teammates must clearly hit the balloon over the line so that their goalies can retrieve them. Once a balloon has been retrieved, the goalie

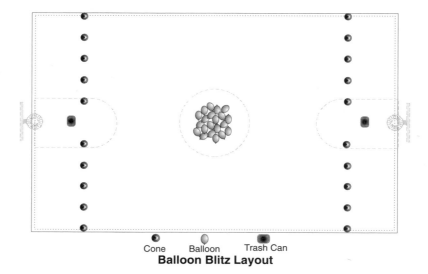

Cone   Balloon   Trash Can
Balloon Blitz Layout

72

immediately drops it into their team's trashcan. This continues until all balloons have been scored.

Advise each team that they may want to have both offensive players and defensive players. Players from each team must decide for themselves what position they want to play. Offensive players for each team try to steal balloons away from their opponents or hit the balloons to their goalies. Defenders, on the other hand, must stand in front of the other team's end line and attempt to bat away any balloons that the opposing goalies are trying to catch.

Scoring

- The team with the most balloons in their trashcan wins that round.
- At the end of class, the teacher can tally up each round to determine the overall Balloon Blitz champion.

Rules and Safety

- Intentionally bumping into other players or using the noodle to hit opponents results in time out from the game!
- Players can change from offense to defense as often as they like.
- Goalies may not cross over their end line to enter the field of play. Balloons may only be retrieved once they are clearly across the end line, whether they are in the air or on the ground. An illegal catch or balloon grab results in an automatic balloon drop into the opposing team's trashcan.
- Only the noodle may be used to touch the balloons. Using hands, by anyone other than the goalie, results in an automatic balloon drop into the opposing team's trashcan.
- Defenders can bat away balloons or block the view of the goalies, but they may not touch the goalies or cross over the end line into the goalie's area.
- Continue play if a balloon pops, then replace it before the next game begins.
- At the end of the round, send the players to their sides and ask the goalies to bring the trashcans to the center so you can count the balloons.

 VARIATION

If available, give everyone except the goalies a scooter. This not only adds a new level of excitement, but it also prolongs each game.

Gator Bait (P-5)

Objective

To improve hand-eye coordination, tossing, shooting, and teamwork skills.

Equipment

- Scooters (1 per person)
- Yarn balls or noodle pieces (at least 100-200; the more the better)
- Different colored jerseys (4-6 sets of each color, or 6-8 sets for classes of 50-65)
- Five-gallon buckets (4-6)
- Enough cones or objects to surround each team's bucket
- Long-handled lollipop paddles (4-6)

Procedure

This is an exciting teamwork game that utilizes scooters and improves shooting and tossing skills. Before classes arrive, put all yarn balls and cut up noodle pieces (the "bait) in the center of the gym. Spread out the buckets, which are each team's home base, randomly around the

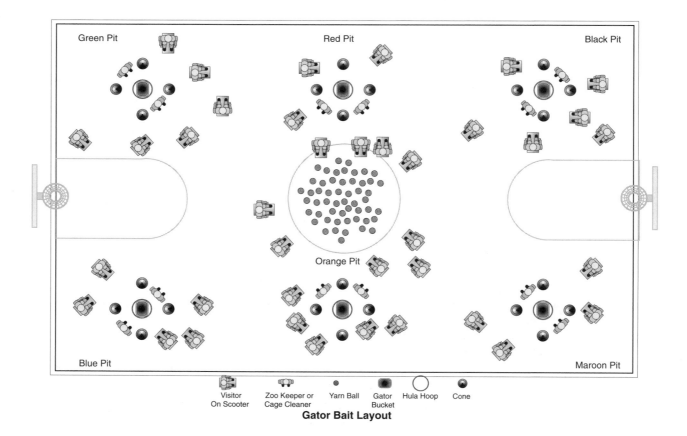

Green Pit   Red Pit   Black Pit

Orange Pit

Blue Pit   Maroon Pit

Visitor On Scooter | Zoo Keeper or Cage Cleaner | Yarn Ball | Gator Bucket | Hula Hoop | Cone

Gator Bait Layout

gym, and encircle each team's bucket with cones to represent "alligator pits" (see Gatorbait layout). Divide the class into four to six different colored teams, 8 to 10 per group (or less, depending on size of class and available equipment). Out of those four to six teams, select one "zookeeper" and one "cage cleaner" to represent each colored team. Have both of them get inside their team's alligator pit. The remaining students are "zoo visitors." For example, if the red team has eight players, then six players represent zoo visitors, one is the zookeeper, and one is the cage cleaner.

At the beginning, all visitors must sit on their scooters outside their team's alligator pit to await further instructions. On the teacher's signal, all visitors take off on their scooters and collect as much bait as they can carry. Visitors then go to any pit but their own to "feed the gators." Visitors feed the gators by tossing or shooting bait from outside the pit boundaries into the bucket. For example, the red team goes to every other team's alligator pits, which have zookeepers and cage cleaners not wearing red jerseys.

Remind the players that visitors do not want to feed their own team's alligator. The zookeeper's job for their assigned alligator pit is to stand around their bucket and swat away all bait being thrown to the alligator. All bait that makes it into the bucket remains. Only the cage cleaners may sweep out the bait that misses the buckets and lands inside the pit boundaries. Cage cleaners use the lollipop paddles to sweep out the bait. Once all or most of the bait has been used up, play stops and the class begins a new game.

Rules and Safety

- No standing on the scooters.
- Visitors must remain on their scooter when tossing bait.
- All visitors must toss bait from outside of opposing team's coned-off alligator pit.

- The team with the least amount of points wins.
- After determining a winner, all bait must be placed back into the center circle.
- If the zookeeper or cage cleaner knocks the bucket over, that team is automatically eliminated for that round.
- Consider grade-level abilities to increase or decrease coned-off boundary circumference.
- Add two alligators (buckets) to each pit.
- Place the cage cleaner on a scooter with a short-handled lollipop paddle.
- Use more than one zookeeper and cage cleaner.
- With kindergarten and first grades, modify the game so that visitors toss bait into *any* alligator pit containing zookeepers and cage cleaners. With this variation, do not worry about team colors or keeping score. Once the buckets are full, empty them into the center, and start over.

VARIATION

When play stops, instruct only the zookeepers and cage cleaners from each pit to total up how much bait their alligator had (that is, how much is in the bucket). The team with the least amount of bait in their bucket wins that round. Total up each round to determine the overall teamwork champ.

Giants, Wizards, Elves, and Dragons (P-5)

Objective

To develop or improve teamwork strategies and cooperation in this aerobic tag game.

Equipment

- Four different colored jerseys (8-15 of each)
- Four different colored hula hoops (1 for each team)

Procedure

Divide the class into four groups. Each group has a designated hoop (their home base) located in one of the corners of the gym. Instruct each group to put on their particular colored jersey, which is inside their designated hoop. Assign each team a name: one group is the Giants, then the Wizards, Elves, and Dragons. Instruct all players that Giants can only tag Wizards; Wizards can only tag Elves; Elves can only tag Dragons; and Dragons can only tag Giants. On a given signal or when the music starts, players must perform some type of locomotor movement (teacher's choice) and attempt to tag their designated targets.

Teammates must form a chain with their other tagged teammates, starting from the center circle and extending all the way to someone standing inside their designated hoop (home base). Once they can touch someone in the home base, the entire team can be set free. A player standing in the home base cannot be tagged, and players forming their chain cannot tag opponents or be tagged.

Rules and Safety

- Only one person may stand in their team's home base.
- Students must move around the gym in the locomotor movement prescribed by the teacher.
- Students must link together in some way—feet to feet, hands to hands, and so on.
- Players may not reenter the game after being tagged until they connect to their team's chain, which must go from the center circle until it reaches home base.

VARIATION

Eliminate the Dragons group if class numbers are too small.

Head Honcho (2-5)

Objective

To practice strategy, honesty, fairness, and honorable sporting behavior. Head Honcho is a fast-paced and exciting game, where a little strategy, luck, and honesty help students to become the Head Honcho. The object of the game is for students to outwit their opponents (or have the best luck) while playing *Rock, Paper, Scissors* (RPS).

Equipment

- Popsicle sticks or tongue depressors (100-200)
- Hula hoops (17 or 34: 17 makes one pyramid for class sizes of 16-35; 34 makes two pyramids for class sizes of 36-70) (Carpet squares or large poly spots can be substituted for hula hoops.)
- Labels, optional (5) (Label each row to eliminate any confusion; I have found that second and third grade students typically get confused about where the rows are.)
- Floor tape or velcro, optional

Procedure

Before students arrive, set up all pyramids (see Head Honcho layout for setup). There are five rows that a player must advance through to become a Head Honcho. All players start in the first row, and they advance up one row every time they win a round of RPS. There must be a minimum of 16 players with a maximum of 30 to 35 players per pyramid. Before the game begins, a teacher should show how to do the three count, *rock, paper,* and *scissors*. Encourage players to play the game to the same rhythm. For example, players must show the symbol on the third count of *1-2-3* or *Head-Honch-O* three count.

Rules and Safety

- Winners of a round must advance one row and find an available hoop.
- Losers of a round must go back one row and find an available hoop. The only exception is when there are more than 16 people in a game. In this case, anyone losing in the first row must go to the end of the line with those waiting to enter the game. The game moves

Bucket of Sticks

Head Honcho Layout

at such a fast pace that players never wait longer than a few seconds. The teacher should stop the game and point out players who are demonstrating honesty and integrity.

■ Remember, students not in one of the first four hoops at the start of the game immediately enter the game once any player advances from the first row.

■ Players waiting in a hoop may leave their hoop to go face off against someone in another hoop in that same row. For example, if there are two players waiting in the first row, but in different hoops, then one player can quickly leave the hoop to join the other so play can resume.

■ All RPS ties result in a do-over until someone wins.

■ Players may not leave their pyramid to go to another pyramid.

HINT

The teacher may allow players who have earned Head Honcho status to start over at another pyramid. Know that this will probably result in one pyramid having more players than the others.

■ Players winning the round in the fifth row, thus becoming a Head Honcho, immediately should go and get one stick out of the bucket. After retrieving a stick, each player should go to the beginning of the pyramid to start over and attempt to be a Head Honcho again. The player with the most sticks at the end of the class is named the Ultimate Head Honcho.

■ Players may have to wait a few seconds sometimes when advancing or going backward because the hoops may already be occupied. In this case, have the students simply wait until the round is finished before they enter the hoop.

■ Players often forget to go back a hoop when they lose because someone is usually ready to face off again in the hoop they are currently occupying. Even if this is the case, they have to go back one hoop.

Outbreak (P-5)

Objective

Outbreak is an exciting new activity that can accompany your foam noodle unit. It guarantees participation, teamwork, and most importantly, an aerobic workout. Outbreak is especially ideal for large classes!

Equipment

■ Foam noodles, at least five feet long (4)

■ Mini-noodles (150 one color, 150 another color; orange and green work well) (Simply cut long noodles into one-to-two-inch mini-noodles; an electric carving knife works best. Yarn balls may be substituted for mini-noodles.)

■ Different colored jerseys (6-10 per group for at least 4-6 groups)

■ Hula hoops (6)

■ Containers to hold mini-noodles (2) (Hockey goals on their backs work great!)

Procedure

A terrible outbreak has spread across the world, and doctors from every nation have been assembled to gather the only cure available to save their countries. It is up to you (the doctors) whether your country survives this terrible outbreak! Divide the students into four to six equal teams. Each team comprises 6 to 10 "doctors" who represent their country by the colored jersey they are wearing (red country, blue country). Each team reports to a designated corner or end of the gym and sits around their "special storage container" (hoop) to wait for instructions (see Outbreak layout). Also choose two to four outbreak "spreaders," who stand in the center circle of the gym, each with a noodle.

To begin, doctors from the red, blue, and orange countries must cross over and retrieve only one orange medicine vial (mini-noodle) from the orange storage area; green, purple, and yellow countries must retrieve only one green medicine vial from the green storage area. Explain that the medicine vials are very fragile, cannot be dropped or thrown, and must be immediately taken to each country's special storage container (kind of like how blood is stored in refrigerators). When the game begins, the doctors begin collecting medicine vials, but the outbreak spreaders begin tagging anyone with their "infectious" noodle, injecting people with the disease. If tagged by a spreader, doctors must stand with legs separated and cannot be set free until a doctor from their own country crawls through their legs.

Rules and Safety

- Only one medicine vial can be carried at a time.
- Doctors must freeze when tagged by a spreader.
- Doctors can only be unfrozen by their own country.
- Spreaders cannot tag a doctor in their country's safe zone. See Outbreak layout for safe zones.
- If anyone is caught cheating, the teacher returns all collected medicine vials to the medicine storage.
- When all or most of the medicine vials have been collected, stop and appoint students from each country to count up their country's total number of medicine vials. The country with the most medicine vials collected for each round or by the end of class saves their population from the outbreak!

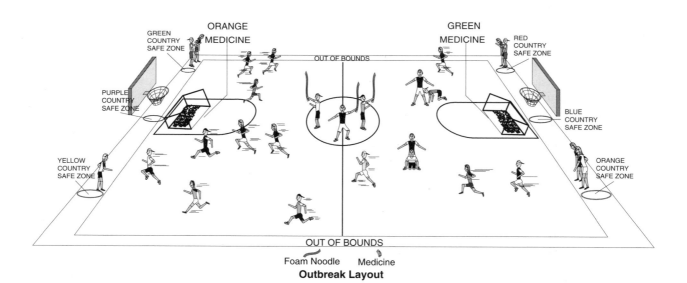

Outbreak Layout

VARIATION

Every round, each team can designate one "spy" who is allowed to go to any of the countries on the other side of the gym and steal one vial of medicine. Once a medicine vial is stolen, a spy returns it to the main storage area. The medicine vials a spy can steal are always a different color from their own team's medicine vials. Appoint a new spy after each round.

Polo Derby (3–5)

Objective

A unique, exhilarating game designed to improve teamwork and cooperation.

Equipment

- Scooters (2-4 per group)
- Gymnastics mats (1 per group; 8-10 mats cover 40 to 50 students)
- Cage/Bigens balls (1 or 2; approximately 36 inches in diameter)
- Different colored jerseys (to represent both teams)

Procedure

If there are eight gymnastics mats, then place four mats on opposite sides of the gym with scooters and jerseys on top. Instruct the class to get into groups of four or five, sit beside one gymnastics mat, and put on their jerseys while waiting for further instructions.

Explain that each group is on one of two opposing teams, depending on whatever color jersey they are wearing and what side of the gym they are on. Each team then assembles their polo derby car by placing their gymnastic mat on top of the scooters provided (see Polo Derby illustration for setup).

Before starting the game, determine which team starts off with the Cage ball by flipping a coin. The object of the game is to advance the Cage ball so that it makes contact with the opposing team's wall. Two players from each team get on top of the mats to ride their polo derby car. The other teammates then push the polo derby car, attempting to hit and advance the Cage ball. When one team hits the opposing team's wall with the Cage ball, a point is scored and a new game begins with new passengers and pushers.

Rules and Safety

- Intentionally crashing into other derby cars or letting go of a derby car is prohibited. Intentional crashes result in a time-out from the game or an automatic point for the other team. Remind each team that if a group has to sit out, they hurt their whole team because they have fewer derby cars in the game.

Polo Derby

- If an unintentional crash occurs causing damage to the polo derby car, then all players of a group must quickly work together to repair their derby car.

- Groups can choose to stay on their side of the gym to defend their wall against a Cage ball, or they can choose to play offense by advancing the Cage ball. After a few games, the teacher should emphasize how students can brainstorm new strategies to be successful. For example, groups can turn the mat sideways and combine with another group to form a huge wall. Challenge the children to think of other strategies.

- Passengers may not have consecutive turns riding the polo derby car. Passengers must become pushers after a team scores a point.

- Cage balls may not be picked up or carried. If a ball gets trapped against the wall, a time-out will be called to move the ball, or the teacher will quickly bump the ball into play.

- Cage balls can be bumped by the polo derby cars and pushed by the passengers. Pushers may only push the polo derby cars. If a passenger kicks a ball, stop the game and award a point to the other team.

- Passengers may not help drive the polo derby cars. Passengers' feet must clearly remain off the ground. They can sit on their knees or pretzel style. Make it clear to pushers that the safety of the passengers is in their hands.

 VARIATION

Allow each team to have goalies who stand at the wall and attempt to keep the Cage ball from making contact.

Allow pushers to kick the ball as long as their hands remain in contact with the polo derby car at all times. If pushers take their hands off the scooter to advance the ball, stop the game and award a point to the other team.

Scooter Scavenger (P-5)

Objective

An invigorating scooter board game that improves teamwork, strategy, and counting skills. There are many exciting variations in this one!

Equipment

- Boxes or buckets (2), containing a variety of items: 15-18 pucks, bean bags, yarn balls, poly spots, short hockey sticks, wiffle balls, golf balls, tennis balls, flags, bowling pins, checkers, or whatever you see fit.
- Scooters (14-18, 1 scooter per group of 2-3)
- All available traffic cones
- Hula hoops (14-18) (One scooter should be placed into each hoop. If possible, match scooter color with hoop color.)

Procedure

Place the grocery store (the box/bucket) containing all of the mentioned items into the center circle of the gym. Divide children into 14 to 18 groups of three or less, and direct each team to go to one of the designated hoops around the gym containing a scooter.

On the teacher's signal, one person from each group performs the specific scooter skill given by the teacher and drives outside all the cones around the perimeter of the gym in the same direction. The Bear Crawl and Seated Relay (forward/backward) usually work best. Once players get back to their starting positions and park their scooters, the goal then is to quickly go to the grocery store to pick one item out of the box. After they place the item into their hoop, the next player can go.

Children really have to communicate and use teamwork or else they might mess up by getting the wrong item from the box. The game continues until the first team is able to retrieve the specified number of items from the grocery store.

Here is a sample format for playing: Before the game begins, the teacher specifies that 10 different items must be collected. Remember, only one item can be collected at a time. Instruct them that they cannot deliver the same type item twice to their hoop. For example, if one player brings back a puck, the following player on the same team should not get another puck because that item has already been selected. Once a round is over, the teacher first awards the winning team (whoever finished the fastest) five bonus points for winning, plus 10 points for the 10 different items for a total of 15 points. The teacher also reveals the bonus item (optional) and adds five points to the team's score if they had it. The teacher then walks around the gym getting totals from each group (they must add their own scores plus any bonuses). The team with the most points at the end of the class wins.

HINT

Although there is a break of action for each child, they all need the rest to catch their breath because *Scooter Scavenger* is a fast-paced, cardiovascular game.

Rules and Safety

- No collisions, reckless driving, or skateboarding will be tolerated.
- Always go in the direction given by the teacher.
- In all variations, only one item from the grocery store can be taken at a time.
- Perform only the scooter skill given by the teacher.
- If a team realizes that they already have a particular item, they cannot take the item back.
- Students will receive a zero if a "mistake" is made when adding up scores. Remind students to count their totals for each round carefully. *Use teamwork!*
- If a group got the same item twice, both items cancel each other out. Neither can be added to the total.

Scooter Boards Football Foam Noodle Nerf Ball Basketball Foam Paddle Yarn Ball Puck Soccer Ball Hockey Stick

Scooter Scavenger Layout

VARIATIONS

Combine teams by the color of hoops. For example, if there are 18 hoops, then place 6 red, 6 blue, and 6 green hoops randomly around the gym. After each round, place totals on a dry-erase board under each team's color (although there will still be individual winners). At the end of class, total up which team color combined has the most points.

Add a twist to the next game by making them get 4 different items, but 3 of each for a total of 12. For example, 3 golf balls, 3 scarves, 3 tennis balls, and 3 checkers. Luck plays a role in this game because some items run out toward the end. If this happens, they must try to find another three of a different item. They cannot, though, count the extra items in their total score.

To really shake things up, consider playing with the objective of finding 7 different items, 2 of each or 2 different items, 7 of each. There are lots of variations, so decide the twist you want to add. Children really have to listen to these instructions and think of their own strategies to win this challenging game!

Skele-Ton of Fun (3-5)

Objective

To implement an exciting, new hands-on approach to learning the skeletal system through the invigorating game of Skele-Ton of Fun.

Equipment

- One sturdy cardboard box or plastic container large enough to hold all sets of bones ("Box of Bones").
- Hula hoop (1 per group) Place the following in each group's hoop: laminated skeletal map of the Poly Bones, clipboard, Fitness Checklist (see page 83), pen or pencil, plastic cup for push-ups, beanbag for sit-ups, basketball, traffic cone, and jump rope.
- Sets of skeletal bone cards (1 or 2) along with a container to place them in. It is best to provide two different colored sets of bone cards to prevent overcrowding at the box, especially with larger classes.
- Basketballs (2)
- Jerseys for the leaders of each group (Important: Choose *reliable* leaders.)
- Skeleton Poly Puzzles (8-10) (See physical education catalogs for an example; 21 pieces are included in one skeleton puzzle set.)

 HINT

Money-saving option: Purchase one Skeleton Poly Puzzle and trace 8-10 complete sets of bones onto various colors of poster board. Cut them out and then laminate them for future use.

Procedure

Skeletal bone cards: In a large font (for easy reading), type each number with the following skeletal information to be printed separately on an 8 1/2 by 11 inch sheet of paper, then taped to poster board, cut out, and laminated.

- Card 1. The **mandible,** which houses your teeth, is connected to the **cranium,** which protects your brain.
- Card 2. Part of your upper vertebrae, the **cervical vertebrae** connects the rib cage to your head.

Fitness Checklist

To earn a card from the center, everyone on your team must perform activity numbers 1 through 13 once. The activities may be performed in any order, but only one activity at a time.

Place a check when each activity is completed.

_____ Activity 1: Push-ups (5 each). Go one at a time and make sure your chest touches the cup.

_____ Activity 2: Partner sit-ups (10). Go two at a time. Each pass of the beanbag counts as one.

_____ Activity 3: Mountain Climbers (10 each). Take turns.

_____ Activity 4: Thread the Needle.

_____ Activity 5: Circle the Circle (with hoop).

_____ Activity 6: Jump rope (10 jumps each). Take turns.

_____ Activity 7: Jog around the gym (2 laps). One at a time; stay close to the wall.

_____ Activity 8: Jumping jacks (30 *together* as a team). Count each one out loud.

_____ Activity 9: Basketball (each person in your group *must* shoot until they make a basketball goal). Only one group may be at one of the two goals at a time.

_____ Activity 10: Squat thrusts (15 *together,* as a team).

_____ Activity 11: Partner jumps with the jump rope (10). Two people at a time.

_____ Activity 12: List the *correct* names of three bones on your skeleton and show to teacher.

1. _____   2. _____   3. _____

_____ Activity 13: Choose any activity from 1-11; perform it again

Card check off:

#1___ #2___ #3___ #4___ #5___ #6___ #7___ #8___ #9___ #10___ #11___ #12___ #13___

- Card 3. The **rib cage** and **sternum** protect the largest and most important muscle in your body—your heart.
- Card 4. Part of your lower vertebrae, the **lumbar vertebrae** attach to the **pelvic girdle.**
- Card 5. The **pelvic girdle,** also known as the "elephant ears," is located at the midpoint of your body.
- Card 6. Connected to the **pelvic girdle,** the left and right **femurs** are the largest bones in the body.
- Card 7. Connected to the **femur,** the left and right **tibias** are the larger of the two bones located in the lower leg. These bones are located between the knees and the ankles.
- Card 8. Known as the smaller of the two leg bones, the left and right **fibulas** are located on the outside of the two lower leg bones. These bones are located between the knees and the ankles.
- Card 9. This grouping of bones that you walk on includes the **calcaneus, tarsals, metatarsals,** and **phalanges.** Hint: There are two of these—your feet.
- Card 10. Known as the largest of the arm bones, the left and right **humerus** are located between your shoulders and elbows.
- Card 11. Connected to the **humerus,** the left and right **radius,** identified as being the thumb-side bones, are the larger of the two bones located in the lower arm.
- Card 12. Known as the smallest arm bones, the left and right **ulna** are located next to the **radius** bone on each arm.
- Card 13. The **carpals, metacarpals,** and **phalanges** make up this body part. Hint: There are two of these and you give high fives with them.

Place the Box of Bones and card boxes in the center of the gym. Set out each hula hoop and place the necessary equipment and materials inside each team's hoop. In the center area of the gym, separate all bones according to their name. For example, place all the femurs in one pile and all of the pelvic girdles in another pile. There should be a total of 13 piles to choose from because there are a total of 13 bone cards.

To begin, instruct students to form even groups of six or eight and send each group to a specific hula hoop on the floor, where they select one group leader. The object of the game is to be the first group to successfully put together a complete skeleton puzzle.

To earn a piece or pieces of the skeleton puzzle, each group must first do the following activities to earn a trip to the bone card box:

1. Perform 1 of the 13 activities from their Fitness Checklist. The group leader is responsible for the checklist.
2. Once an activity has been completed from the checklist, the leader checks it off.
3. The leader then gets a bone card from the bone card box.
4. The group must then read and figure out which bone the bone card is describing. Remind students to check each card number off at the bottom of the checklist so that it is not chosen again.
5. Immediately after figuring out which bone is being described, the leader may go and select that bone (or both bones if left and right bones are involved) from the Box of Bones.
6. Each group places its pieces of the skeleton puzzle on the floor, looks at its skeletal map, and puts the pieces together. Then they determine which activities they need to do and which bones they need.

HINT

Again, it is important to check off the bone card numbers so that their leader does not accidentally retrieve that same card again.

7. The groups continue this format until they have performed all 13 activities and collected all the bones to successfully form a complete 21-piece skeleton, like the one on their skeletal map.

8. If the leader brings back the wrong bone or a bone that has been already collected, the group must redo the same activity from the Fitness Checklist. Once the activity has been completed, the leader returns the bone for a new one.

The class concludes by holding up each bone to review its name and where it is located in the body. Emphasize the importance of teamwork and how crucial it is in playing the game and in life.

This activity is optional, but it works well when implemented before playing Skele-Ton of Fun. The children participate in it for the sole purpose of familiarizing and reviewing each bone's name and location.

Procedure: Place 13 hula hoops randomly all over the gym. Inside each hoop, place a piece or all pieces of a particular bone. For example, place all of the femurs in one hoop and all of the pelvic girdles in another hoop. There should be a total of 13 hoops to choose from because there is a total of 13 bone cards used in Skele-Ton of Fun.

Also place inside each hula hoop the bone card that explains those particular bones or grouping of bones. Optional: Place a picture of the skeleton map inside each hula hoop with the bones highlighted. This provides students with a visual location of the particular bone being described and exactly where it is located in the body.

To begin, hand out a labeled skeleton map and instruct students to visit each of the 13 hula hoops. They do not have to visit the hula hoops in any particular order. At each station they must look at the bone, read the bone card, look at the map for its highlighted location (if provided), and fill in the blank on their handout with the name of the bone. Students may visit each hoop as often as they wish. Encourage them to ask a teacher if they have questions or need assistance.

At the end of class, review each bone with the class as you (or selected students) put the skeleton puzzle together.

Rules and Safety

- Only one fitness activity from the checklist can be performed at a time.
- Only the chosen leader may go and get a bone card or go to the Box of Bones to collect a bone.
- The leaders for each group are responsible for making sure no one cheats and that all activities are successfully completed.
- If anyone is caught cheating, the teacher may take away one or more bones from a group and return them to the Box of Bones.
- Only one bone (unless it involves a left and right bone) may be taken from the Box of Bones at a time.
- Groups may only take the bones being described on the bone card. If the wrong bone is selected, their checklist will reflect this mistake at the conclusion of the game. If the teacher catches the mistake, the bone is returned and the teacher explains the mistake to that team.

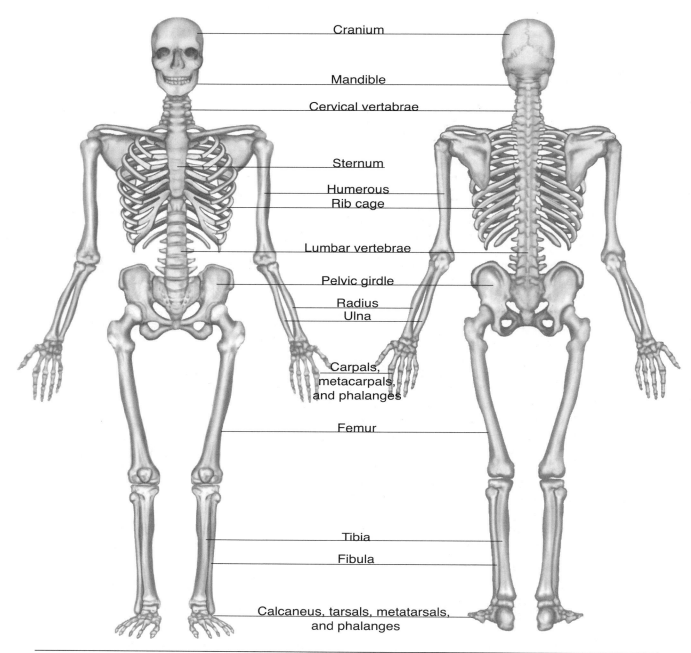

Cranium

Mandible

Cervical vertabrae

Sternum

Humerous
Rib cage

Lumbar vertebrae

Pelvic girdle

Radius
Ulna

Carpals,
metacarpals,
and phalanges

Femur

Tibia

Fibula

Calcaneus, tarsals, metatarsals,
and phalanges

From *No Standing Around in My Gym* by J.D. Hughes, 2003, Champaign, IL: Human Kinetics. Adapted, by permission, from National Strength Conditioning Association, 2000, The Biomechanics of Resistance Exercise. In *Essentials of Strength Training*, edited by T.R. Baechle and R.W. Earle (Champaign, IL: Human Kinetics), 27.

Sonic Boom (3-5)

Objective

A large group activity (45-70) designed to enhance teamwork, offensive and defensive strategy, and cardiovascular endurance.

Equipment

- Folding gymnastics mats (at least 6-10)
- Cage balls or Bigens balls (2 or 3, at least 36-inch)

- Scooters (1 for each person)
- Two different colored jerseys (to distinguish each team).

Procedure

Stand up three to five mats on each side of the gym (see Sonic Boom layout for setup). Divide the class into two teams and have them sit on their side of the gym. Scenario: You all live in outer space. Your team lives on one of two planets. There is a Team 1 and a Team 2. You can decide on your team names. Each planet is protected from "meteors" (Bigens balls) by "force fields" (mats). The object of the game is to try and destroy all of the other team's force fields by knocking them down.

Before the game begins, each student must decide whether to be an astronaut, android, or both. Astronauts protect the force fields; androids eliminate the force fields. The game begins by a throw-in of the Bigens balls by the teacher. Astronauts (three or four per force field) sit on their scooters and move around their team's force fields, protecting their force field with hands and feet from the huge meteors being pushed or kicked by the androids on the other team. Astronauts and androids may not touch the force fields with their hands. Androids from each team move around on their scooters, pushing or kicking the meteors in the direction of the opposing team's force fields on the other side of the gym. Once a force field is down, it stays down.

Rules and Safety

- Meteors may be stopped and pushed, but not transported.
- Neither astronauts nor androids may place their hands on a force field.
- All players must remain seated on their scooters at all times.

VARIATION

Not enough scooters for everyone? Allow two to four astronauts to stand in front of their force fields, or have all androids crabwalk—whatever works best for your class.

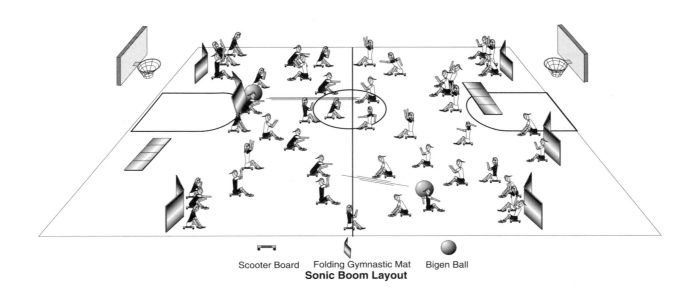

Scooter Board   Folding Gymnastic Mat   Bigen Ball
Sonic Boom Layout

Swamp Ball (P-2)

Objective

A great cardiovascular game that not only improves hand-eye coordination, throwing, catching, and aiming skills, but also introduces and reinforces young children to teamwork, cooperative, and strategical skills.

Equipment

- Yarn balls or similarly lightweight objects (enough to easily fill two five-gallon buckets)
- Tall traffic cones (to represent both sides of the swamp)
- Five-gallon buckets (2-4)
- Green scooters (2) and green jerseys (2) to represent the alligators, optional

Procedure

Scatter all yarn balls and other round objects evenly throughout the gym. Divide the class into two teams and have each team stand on opposite ends of the gym. Select two students to each get a jersey and a scooter and go inside the alligator pit (the alligator pit is between the traffic cones; see Swamp Ball layout).

Explain that they are in a swamp and in this swamp is an alligator pit. For all the children to make it safely out of the swamp, all children must use teamwork by throwing the yarn balls over the alligator pit into the hands of a friend on the other side. When a yarn ball is caught, the player immediately takes it to a bucket against the wall on the side it is caught. Each side continues this process until every ball is either in a bucket or stuck inside the alligator pit. The teacher then counts how many yarn balls were stuck in the alligator pit and collected by the two alligators in the buckets. There are usually a lot of yarn balls in the pit the first few games because children simply pick up and throw balls wildly over the pit without trying to throw to someone.

Challenge the children, really emphasizing teamwork, to see if they can get less in the pit and more in the hands of their teammates across from them. Explain that one simple strategy, which involves teamwork, is to get a friend's attention before throwing the ball over the pit—once you have it, give your a friend a nice and easy throw. Another strategy is to stay spread out and not crowd one area when throwing and catching the yarn balls.

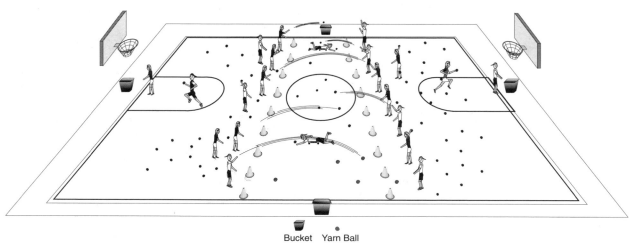

Bucket   Yarn Ball
Swamp Ball Layout

Rules and Safety

- Only one yarn ball can be picked up and thrown at a time.
- Once a ball lands inside the alligator pit, it must remain there.
- Nothing can enter the alligator pit (arms, hands, feet).
- If a yarn ball hits the ground, it may not be placed into the bucket. It can, though, be picked up and thrown again.

VARIATIONS

Select more students—or even a teacher!—on scooters to be the alligators.

Time each game and challenge them to beat their existing record by getting less yarn balls stuck in the pit than the times before.

Switch and Vicious Volleyball (3-5)

Objective

To reinforce volleyball skills of bumping and setting in the game situations of Switch Volleyball and Vicious Volleyball. Note: These indoor activities are designed for 25 to 40 children. If two teachers are available, it is best to combine these games with an outdoor game, especially if the class is large.

Equipment

- Nets (2)
- Base (1)
- Oversized beach balls or volleyball trainers (2-4)

Procedure

Set up each game using half of the gym. Divide the class into two groups, Group A and Group B. Assign Group A to one side of the gym (Switch Volleyball) and Group B to the other side (Vicious Volleyball). After you give instructions for each game, start the games and switch sides after 15 to 20 minutes of play.

- Station 1: Switch Volleyball—The object of this game is to stay on the serving side the longest. Divide the group into three teams. Team 1 is on the serving side. Team 2 is on the other side. Team 3 waits to play on the side. The serving side has a designated serving base. Team 1 starts the game by standing on the service base to serve the ball (with one hit) over the net. After the serve, there are unlimited hits to get the ball back over the net; however, the same student cannot hit the ball two times in a row.

  ❑ Rotation: (1) The team waiting to play always enters the game on the nonserving side. (2) If the serving team wins the point, they stay and the other team goes to the sideline. (3) If the nonserving team wins the point, they go under the net to the serving side. The team that was on the serving side goes to the sideline, and the team on the sideline enters the game. (See diagram on page 90 for further clarification.)

  ❑ How to win a point: The opponent's ball lands on the ground or goes out of bounds (on the line is inbounds). The same person on the opponent's team hits the ball two times in a row.

- Station 2: Vicious Volleyball—Divide the group into two teams. The goal for each team is to seize all of the opposing team's players. This is accomplished by legally throwing the ball or bumping the ball over the net in such a way that it cannot be returned. When the ball hits the ground, throwers are awarded the opportunity to bring someone new to their side or save friends by calling them back over to their side. The next serve goes to the team who lost a player. Start a new game once a team gets everyone on their side or when all but two or three players are left on one side.

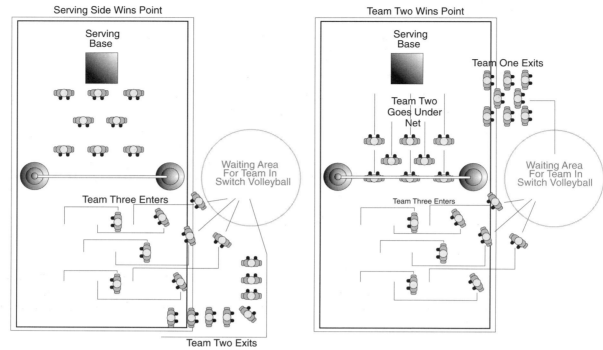

Switch Volleyball Layout

Rules and Safety

- ■ Absolutely no dropping the ball on purpose.
- ■ The ball must clear the net each time.

VARIATION

Add one or two more beach balls or volleyball trainers to Vicious Volleyball. This requires lots of concentration and takes the game to a new level of fun.

Team Trashball (P-5)

Objective

Team Trashball is an excellent cooperative game designed to improve students' throwing, catching, and scooter board skills (optional), while improving problem solving, teamwork, communication skills, and cardiovascular fitness. (See Team Trashball layout on page 91 for setup.)

VARIATION

Team Trashball can be played with or without scooters. Scooters add an extra level of difficulty and make the game longer to play.

Equipment

- ■ Scooter (1 per person)
- ■ Different colored jerseys (to represent each team) (2 sets)
- ■ Storage bins without lids (6)
- ■ Five-gallon buckets (2-4)
- ■ Yarn balls (100; ideally, 50 yellow yarn balls in one bin and 50 white in another bin)

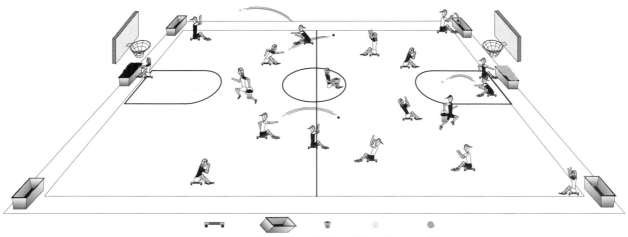

Scooter Board   Storage Bin   5 Gallon   Yellow Yarn   Black Yarn
                                Bucket   Ball   Ball
Team Trashball Layout

Procedure

Before class begins, place one storage bin in each corner of the gym. Fill the other two storage bins with yarn balls and place them in the middle of those storage bins at the end of the gym (see layout). Divide the class into two teams and send them to opposite sides of the gym to sit on a scooter (optional) and put on the colored jersey their team will represent. Select one or two players from each team to be the "Ball Hounds." Each Ball Hound gets a five-gallon bucket and sits in the middle of the gym.

To begin: On the signal "go," students may start taking balls, one at a time, out of their middle storage bin to toss to teammates. Remember, each team may only get the designated colored yarn ball from the storage bin behind their team. The object of the game is to for each team to successfully transfer their yarn balls into the corner storage bins at the opposite side of the gym using any strategy within the rules.

Rules and Safety

■ Once players have possession of a ball, they cannot move forward or backward on the scooter. They must immediately pass or shoot the ball. Players in possession of balls may move clockwise or counterclockwise.

■ A Ball Hound may only pick up any ball that lands on the ground. The Ball Hounds' job is to pick up only those balls dropped by their team. They put them in their bucket and quickly return them to their team's storage bin.

■ All balls must be thrown, not handed off.

■ Players must remain on scooters at all times. If catching a ball results in players falling off, they must immediately drop the ball.

■ The first team to completely get all their team's yarn balls to the bins on the other side is declared the winner.

 HINT

Emphasize the use of strategies. Remind them that strategies are great for improving performance and give their team a better chance to win. Examples of strategies include using an assembly line approach from the bin containing their team's yarn balls to one or both of the empty bins across the gym. Encourage students to form groups of two to three to toss and catch all the way down to their team's bin.

Toxic Blast (P-5)

Objective

To improve teamwork, throwing accuracy, and strategic skills in the exhilarating game of Toxic Blast.

Equipment

- Traffic cones, or some form of boundary for both teams
- Bigens balls (1 or 2)
- Gatorskin or Nerf balls (30-50)
- Different colored jerseys (2 sets of 3)

Procedure

Place traffic cones five yards from each side of the centerline of the gym. Divide the class into two teams and send them to opposite sides of the gym. Select three players from each team to represent the "Toxic Clean-Up Crew." These players must wear the assigned colored jerseys, which also designate their team. The Toxic Clean-Up Crew's jobs are to gather balls that get stuck between both boundaries and give them to their teammates. Divide the balls and place half on each side of the gym. Place both Bigens balls ("Toxic Waste Balls") in the center of the gym. (See Toxic Blast layout for setup.)

Explain that on the teacher's signal, each team picks up the balls on their side of the gym and begins throwing or rolling the Gatorskin balls directly at the Toxic Waste balls. The object of the game is to hit the Toxic Waste balls enough times to propel them into the other team's boundary. If a ball hits a team's boundary, then a fatal toxic waste spill occurs and the game is over. Place both balls in the center to begin a new round. The team with the most points at the end of class is declared the teamwork winner.

Rules and Safety

- Gatorskin balls may only be thrown at the Toxic Waste balls.
- Players must stay on their side of the gym behind their team's cones at all times.
- Anyone entering between the boundaries other than the Toxic Clean-Up Crew immediately loses that team's round. In other words, no one can reach in and get a ball from the middle.

Bucket   Yarn Ball
Toxic Blast Layout

- Anyone touching the Toxic Waste balls loses the round for that team (including accidental contact by the Toxic Clean-Up Crew or throwers).
- After each round, the Toxic Clean-Up Crew must select players from their team to take their spots.

HINT

You may want to let them figure this out: Placing balls in front of a moving Toxic Waste ball alters its direction and can move it away from a team's boundary.

VARIATION

Increase or decrease the gap between each team depending on age and ability levels.

Treasure Quest (P-5)

Objective

Treasure Quest is an exciting new scooter activity that can accompany your scooter unit. It guarantees participation, teamwork, and most importantly, an aerobic workout. Treasure Quest is especially ideal for large classes.

Equipment

Equipment needs for Treasure Quest and Outbreak are very similar. The following is for a class of 50 to 60 students. Simply add or decrease equipment based on each class's size.

- Mini-noodles (100-150 one color, 100-150 another color; orange and green work well) (Simply cut long noodles into one-to-two-inch mini-noodles; an electric carving knife works best. Yarn balls or beanbags may be substituted for noodles. The more treasure, the longer each game lasts.)
- Containers to hold mini-noodles (2) (hockey goals on their backs work great)
- Different colored jerseys, if possible (7 sets, 6 sets for teams and one set for the Sea Pirates; get a little creative and give them eye patches or pirate hats)
- Eight hula hoops, buckets, or containers (Containers work best because when the game is over, it is easy to transfer treasure back to the treasure chests. Sea Pirates also need two buckets to place their stolen treasure in.)
- Scooters for each team. There should be one less scooter than the number of players per group. For example, if one team has 8 players, then they need 7 scooters.
- One scooter and foam noodle or soft tagging device per Sea Pirate.

Procedure

The world's greatest countries are on a voyage to obtain all the gold (mini-noodles) in the world, each realizing that the wealthiest country can achieve world dominance. Each country needs to beware of the mighty wrath of the ongoing Sea Pirates, who are out to steal the gold from each team's Mother Ship (hula hoop or container).

Before class begins, place scooters and jerseys inside each of the six containers or hula hoops (see Treasure Quest layout on page 94 for placement of all other equipment). Divide the class into six equal teams when the students arrive. Each team comprises 6 to 10 Explorers who represent their country by the colored jersey they are wearing. Teams report to their designated corner and sit around their container to wait for instructions. The one teammate from each group who does not get a scooter is that team's Rescuer. Note: Additional Rescuers may be needed to avoid players being frozen too long. Add one or two more Rescuers with classes of 50 or more.

Next, choose four to six Sea Pirates who sail the waters. Each pirate needs a rowboat (scooter) and a foam noodle (or some other tagging device). Switch Pirates every 5 to 10 minutes.

To begin, explain that the goal of the game is for each Mother Ship to collect as much treasure as possible. Explain that Explorers from the red, blue, and orange Mother Ships must sail on their rowboats to retrieve only one colored treasure (e.g., orange) from the treasure chest located on the opposite side of the gym. Green, purple, and yellow countries, as well, must retrieve only one colored treasure (e.g., green) from the treasure chest located on the opposite side of the gym. All treasure must be immediately taken and put in their Mother Ship's treasure chest (container).

When the game begins, the Explorers begin collecting treasure, and the Sea Pirates begin tagging with their noodle Explorers who are carrying treasure. The Sea Pirates' objective is to steal back any treasure taken from the treasure chests. Sea Pirates must immediately put any stolen treasure into their buckets, and they may not tag anyone else until they have put their treasure away. Explorers that are tagged by a Sea Pirate must give their treasure to the Sea Pirate, then immediately freeze in that spot. Encourage Explorers to wave their hands frantically to get a Rescuer's attention. Tagged Explorers cannot be set free until the Rescuer from their own country comes to save them. Rescuers simply walk over to their frozen teammates on the scooter and drag them by their feet all the way back to their Mother Ship. At this point, the Rescuer and Explorer must switch roles, and teams continue this process throughout the entire game. This way, everyone gets opportunities to be Rescuers and Explorers.

Scoring

■ When all or most of the treasure has been collected, stop and appoint one student from each Mother Ship to count up their country's total number of treasure. The country with the most treasure collected for each round or by the end of class achieves world dominance! Note: Pirates can also be declared the winners if they have the most treasure.

Rules and Safety

■ An Explorer or a Sea Pirate can take only one treasure at a time.

■ Explorers must clearly carry their treasure in their hand and freeze when tagged by a Sea Pirate. The Explorer must immediately give the treasure to the Pirate.

■ Explorers can only be unfrozen by a Rescuer from their own country. Rescuers should be on the lookout for teammates who are frozen and waving their hands in the air. Rescuers can drag only one frozen teammate by the feet at a time to the Mother Ship.

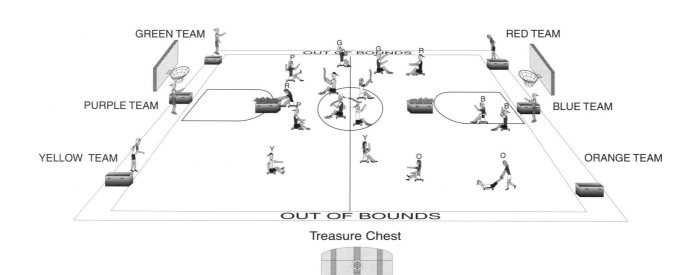

Treasure Chest

- Rescuers, once they save a teammate, must switch roles and become an Explorer for their team.
- Sea Pirates cannot tag an Explorer while they are at their Mother Ship.
- Sea Pirates can only tag Explorers who are carrying treasure. Pirates may not tag anyone else until they take the stolen treasure back to one of their buckets.
- If a team is caught cheating, the teacher collects and returns all their treasure to the treasure chest.
- Explorers can ride their scooters forward or backward. Remind students to always watch where they are going, especially when moving backward. The teacher can change this if necessary.

 VARIATION

Every round, each team can designate one "Spy" who is allowed to go to any of the countries on the other side of the gym and steal one piece of treasure. Once the treasure is stolen, a spy returns it to the appropriate treasure chest. Stolen treasure must always be a different color from their own team's treasure; otherwise, spies might be tempted to take it to their Mother Ship. It is the responsibility of each team to appoint a new spy after each round.

Traditional Games With a New Twist

The following games will be familiar to many of your students. You can make physical education even more exciting by adding a new twist to traditional games.

Bowling Bombs (P-5)

Objective

To improve bowling or rolling accuracy and cardiovascular fitness. To encourage teamwork and group awareness (teams have to be aware not to knock down their own pins!).

Equipment

- Bowling pins (36-40, 9 or 10 per quadrant)
- Soft touch or Gatorskin balls (20-40)
- Traffic cones (to section off each quadrant)

Procedure

Each group, designated with a color and sectioned off into four teams, has a number of pins set up in their quadrant that they must guard (see the Bowling Bombs layout out on page 96). Explain that when the game begins, each team must attempt to knock down the opposing team's pins while at the same time guarding their own pins. All teams must stay in their own quadrants. Teams must try to knock down the other team's pins by performing underhand rolls. Instruct them that once a pin has been knocked down, it must stay down, even if your own team accidentally knocks it down. The team that has the most pins standing after a designated time limit (or has the only pins standing) wins!

Rules and Safety

- The ball has to clearly be bowled or rolled underhanded.
- No crossing over into another team's quadrant.
- Once a pin is down, it stays down.
- No more than two players may guard a pin.
- No straddling a pin or putting your feet around a pin.
- Once a team's pins are all down, they may still continue bowling until the game is over.

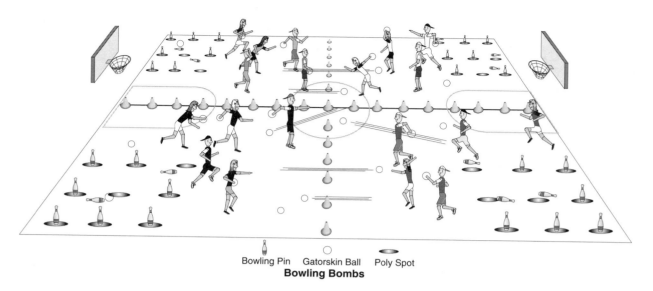

Bowling Pin   Gatorskin Ball   Poly Spot
Bowling Bombs

 HINT

To speed the setup process for the next game, place round poly spots on the floor to designate pin placement.

Color Germ Tag (P-2)

Objective

To reinforce basic locomotor movements, especially when combined with the Body Awareness and Movement Exploration Unit in chapter 1 (page 22).

Equipment

- Jerseys (6-8 per team) (a different color for each team)
- Hoop (1 for each team)
- Music (to add more fun and energy)

Procedure

Color Germ Tag is modified from the original game of Germ Tag, where students try to avoid being tagged by fleeing and dodging the Germs. Count students off and send them to a designated hula hoop in the gym, where each must put on the colored jersey lying inside the hoop. Each hoop should have the same number of jerseys. Next, instruct all students to sit down for further instructions.

Explain that one team is selected as the Germs (who are "It") and must go to the center of the gym. Once the teacher gives the signal or the music begins, the other teams, along with the Germs, must perform a locomotor movement such as hop, skip, jump, or gallop around the gym while the Germs try to tag them. Once tagged by a Germ, players must stand frozen, legs apart with their hands waving in the air, until someone from their team crawls under their legs. Teams also can avoid being tagged by lying on their backs and wiggling their arms and legs wildly in the air. While lying on their backs and wiggling, the Germs cannot tag them. After a designated time limit or when one or two songs are over, choose the fastest team to sit down in personal space and get quiet—they get to be the next Germs.

Rules and Safety

- Only the team selected as Germs may tag others.
- The only way to become unfrozen is for another student to crawl through their legs.
- Everyone, including the Germs, must perform the locomotor movement as prescribed by the teacher.

Cross Over Craze (P-5)

Objective

To teach strategy and teamwork. To encourage continual movement and hand-eye coordination.

Equipment

- Colored jerseys (a different color per quadrant, 1 per student)
- As many soft, lightweight balls or swim noodles that you have—the more the better!
- Traffic cones to section off each quadrant

Procedure

Cross Over Craze is an excellent strategic and teamwork-oriented game that will have your students moving around so much that even they won't know where they are going. The object of the game is to keep all of your teammates together and get all opposing players into your team's quadrant. Divide the class into four groups as evenly as possible, and assign them a color quadrant (see Cross Over Craze layout). Disperse all balls evenly over the gym. On the teacher's signal, students begin rolling Gatorskin balls, yarn balls, or lightweight balls at opposing teams in the other three quadrants (foam noodles are also fun to use). When a ball hits a player, that player must cross over into the section from which the ball came. This process continues for a designated amount of time or until most players end up in one quadrant.

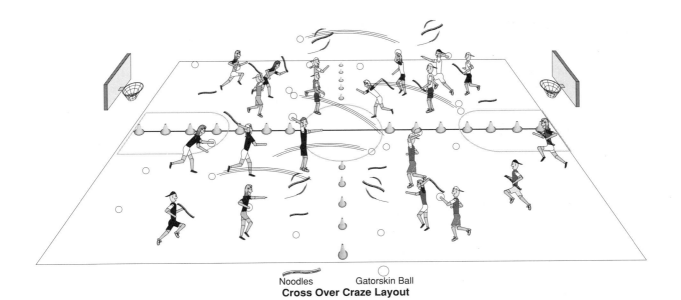

Noodles   Gatorskin Ball
Cross Over Craze Layout

97

Rules and Safety

- When they are hit or when their balls are caught, players must immediately go to that opposing team's quadrant.
- A player can get hit multiple times and continually cross from quadrant to quadrant. Remind students that when they hit someone, they should point to them because sometimes players don't know where the ball came from.

HINT

You may want to let them figure this out! Once they enter the new quadrant, someone from his or her own team can roll and hit them to get them back to their side.

VARIATION

Increase difficulty by eliminating any throwing of the balls.

Dr. Feelgood (P-5)

Objective

Dr. Feelgood is a nonstop, cardiovascular game, which involves fleeing and dodging to stay out of the "hospital." Students roll Gatorskin balls across the gym floor attempting to contact the opposing team's players.

Equipment

- Scooters (6-8)
- Different colored jerseys (4-6 per group)
- Traffic cones (to mark off hospital area)
- Gatorskin balls (30-50) (the more the better)
- Yarn balls (these may be more appropriate for the younger children)

Procedure

Divide the class into two teams, one team on each side of the gym (see Dr. Feelgood layout on page 99 for setup). Three or four "doctors" need to be chosen for each team. They immediately go to the hospital to put on a colored jersey and retrieve an "ambulance" (scooter).

To begin, the teacher gives the signal, and each team starts rolling Gatorskin balls. Once hit, the students must immediately sit down and call out something like "Dr. Feelgood, come save me." One of the doctors then drives out to the players needing medical assistance and places them on the ambulance to take back to the hospital. Once at the hospital, the injured players must "heal" themselves by performing 10 to 20 repetitions of their favorite exercise (jumping jacks, for example). The teacher may want to decide which exercises work best.

Rules and Safety

- Anyone who gets hit by a rolled object must sit down and wait for a doctor.
- Students must ride on the ambulance all the way to the hospital.
- Students must heal themselves by performing 10 to 20 repetitions of their favorite exercise before reentering the game.
- Absolutely no throwing of the Gatorskin balls! Balls must be rolled.

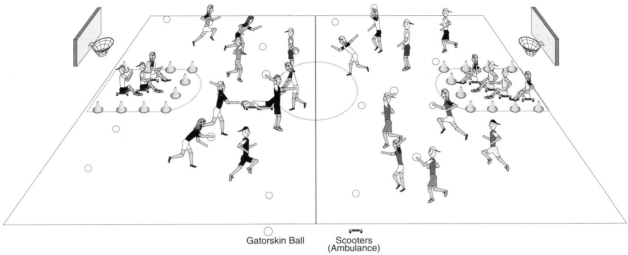

Gatorskin Ball   Scooters
                   (Ambulance)
Dr. Feelgood Layout

VARIATIONS

When doctors get hit while rescuing someone, they too must immediately go back to the hospital and do 10 to 20 jumping jacks before reentering.

Or, if the doctors get hit, they must sit down until another doctor comes to save them.

Frisbee Frenzy (3-5)

Objective

To improve Frisbee throwing accuracy, strategy, and teamwork.

Equipment

- Hula hoops (10-12)
- Frisbees (10-12)
- Tennis balls (10-12)
- Traffic cones (10-12)

Procedure

Frisbee Frenzy is a fast-paced and cooperative game. If possible, divide children into 10 to 12 equal groups of three and send them to one of the 10 to 12 hoops on the ground. (See Frisbee Frenzy layout on page 100 for class setup.) Each team must start from inside of their hoop.

To begin, the teacher gives the signal "go." The first person in line picks up the Frisbee, and the second person in line runs toward the cone on the other side of the field and stops. The first person in line then throws the Frisbee to the second player. When the Frisbee is caught, the player who caught it must stop and pivot toward the cone at the end of the line. The third person in line runs past the second person and stops to try and catch the Frisbee once again.

The object of this game is for each team to continue moving the Frisbee down the field until they get to their end line, designated by a final cone that has a tennis ball resting on it. Once at the end line, the student with the Frisbee must make a choice: throw the Frisbee at the cone to attempt to knock the tennis ball off or make one more throw to a partner to get it as close as possible to the cone to make a safer and easier throw to knock the ball off. Either way, if they miss and the Frisbee hits the ground, the team must start over.

Frisbee Frenzy Layout

Rules and Safety

- Whenever the Frisbee hits the ground, the three players must start over from their hoop.
- The first team to knock over the tennis ball must stand together waving their hands to acknowledge they won: first place gets five points; second place is awarded three points; and third place is awarded one point.
- The teacher, at any time, can award a "Double Points" round for the winners of that particular round.
- At the end of each round, blow the whistle to tell students to immediately go back to their hoops to start again.
- Continue until the end of class. The team with the most points wins.
- If a team is unsuccessful, the teacher at any time can move a team's hoop closer to the cone. Or, if a team is dominating each round, the teacher can move their hoop farther away.

HINTS

Don't stand too close to your partner to catch the Frisbee. The quicker you can get the Frisbee down the field, the better chance your team has to win or score.

Also, don't get too far away from the person throwing the Frisbee. If too far, it is extremely tough to catch the Frisbee. Not too far and not too close—remember to find a happy medium.

Emphasize teamwork! It's what we're all about.

VARIATION

Combine teams by hoop color. To get an overall score, add each team's total together. At the end of class, tell which team won.

Game Creations (3-5)

Objectives

To enhance critical thinking, social skills, and creativity skills. To let the children experiment with brainstorming and creating new games.

Equipment

■ Whatever each group chooses—as long as it is inside the equipment room!

Procedure

Here is an idea that you won't see often, but the children will love (and don't be surprised if some of your students make up a game that you want to try in class!). Let students select their own groups, which must have at least four to eight members. Inform each group that they must think of and agree on a unique game (never been done before in class) and that they must come up with a name, a set of rules, safety guidelines, instructions on how to play, and possible variations. Only one member for each group may go into the equipment room to get equipment for their game. If equipment is not being used, students must return it to its proper place before being issued any more equipment.

Introduce each group's game at the end of class or at the end of the week. Inform each group that their ideas may be graded and that the teacher may use some games in a future physical education class. At the end of the week, each group demonstrates their game in front of the class. Consider awarding certificates or trophies for the best ideas.

Rules and Safety

■ Play in your own area.

■ Each group must record their game on paper.

■ Each group is given a pass to go into equipment room (one at a time).

VARIATION

Use this activity as an assessment or a homework assignment. Instruct students to answer the questions from the list.

1. Is it a sport, dance, or fitness activity?
2. What skills will be used?
3. Where is the best place to play the activity?
4. What are the boundaries?
5. Is this an individual, partner, group, or team game?
6. How many can play?
7. What equipment is needed?
8. How do you set it up? (draw a diagram)
9. What are the direction to play?
10. What are the rules and safety precautions?

Iceberg! (P-3)

Objective

To develop and enhance trust, teamwork, and listening skills.

Equipment

■ Scooters and blindfolds (1 each for every pair of students)

■ As many traffic cones, mats, boxes, buckets, or any other obstacles that are available

■ Small plastic boats (4-6) (Boats can be found at most dollar stores; write *Titanic* on each boat.)

Procedure

Scatter cones, mats, boxes, and buckets (the "icebergs") all over gym. Make sure to place all boats under the traffic cones before the children arrive. Students choose a partner and they share

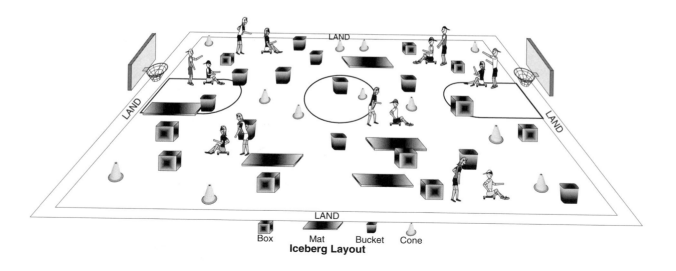

Box · Mat · Bucket · Cone
Iceberg Layout

one scooter and one blindfold. Students then gather on one end of the gym to wait for further instructions.

Start by asking children if they know the fatal story about the Titanic and how it sunk. Most children are able to answer this question; summarize any details, if necessary. Explain that they do not want to end up like the Titanic and that today they must use good communication and listening skills to maneuver through the "ocean" (the gym) and avoid the icebergs—or they too will sink! There are three versions that students can play during the class.

Version A: All "ships" (children on scooters) put a blindfold on and must be verbally directed through the ocean of icebergs by the captains (their partners). Any group that crashes into an iceberg must immediately go back and start over every time. If a group makes it safely across the ocean, the captain and ship switch positions and continue back across the ocean.

Version B: In this version, the captain wears the blindfold and pushes the ship through the ocean of icebergs while listening to the ship's verbal commands. Same rules apply as in version A.

Version C: Follow same procedure as in version B, but this time each group represents the Carpathia. (Ask the children if they know about the Carpathia, the boat that rescued the Titanic survivors.) This is where the hidden boats are used. Explain that each team is allowed to turn over one "iceberg" (cone) to try to uncover one of the Titanics. If a Titanic is rescued, carry it to safety once again while managing not to hit any other obstacles. With younger children, we usually let them turn over as many cones as they can until they find all the Titanics.

Rules and Safety

- In version A, the captain cannot touch the ship; only verbal commands may be given.
- In version B, the captain cannot let go of the partner.
- Collisions with icebergs always result in starting over.
- Blindfolds must stay on at all times (no peeking!).
- Ships that crash into other ships must start over.
- Ships that hit land must start over.

Pin Bombardment (P-5)

Objective

An exciting game that focuses on developing teamwork, strategy, rolling, and underhand throwing skills.

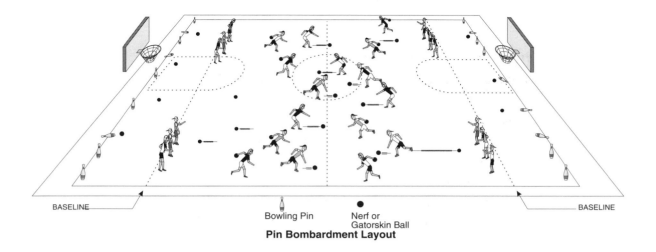

BASELINE _____   BASELINE

Bowling Pin   Nerf or
                 Gatorskin Ball

Pin Bombardment Layout

Equipment

- Bowling pins (16-20, 8-10 per side)
- Gatorskin balls, round Nerf balls, or lightweight round balls (all balls available to program)

Procedure

Set up all pins behind each baseline of the gym, and place all balls in the center circle (see Pin Bombardment layout for setup). Separate the class into two teams, one team at each baseline. The object of the game is to roll or throw balls underhanded in an attempt to knock all of the opposing team's bowling pins over. Each team, though, can defend their pins from where they are standing by knocking balls away or by standing on the baseline in front of their pins (kind of like making a human wall). Their feet cannot go past the baseline.

A winner is declared once all pins are knocked over. An alternative way to play is to see who has the most pins standing after a predetermined time limit.

Rules and Safety

- Players must stay on their side of the gym.
- No throwing overhand or throwing at players!
- Once a pin is down, it stays down.
- Once a ball has stopped rolling, a player may get it from behind the baseline.
- To get past human walls, balls can be rolled at and played off the walls.
- No kicking the balls.
- If rules are broken or if deemed necessary, the teacher may knock over pins.
- Players may not cross over center line.

 HINTS

Keep all balls, then charge the other team, bombarding them with lots of balls. It's easier to defend a few balls as opposed to a whole lot of balls.

Each team should decide who will be rollers and who will make human walls to protect their team's pins.

Try ricocheting balls off the walls to hit the pins.

Who's Who in PE? (3-5)

Objective

To give all children at the beginning of the year an activity to learn names and get to know their class while engaging in a goofy game.

Equipment

- Who's Who sheets and pencils (1 per person)
- Jump ropes (6-8 each)
- Hula hoops (6-8 each)
- Basketballs and Buddy Walkers™ (4 each)
- Scarves, yarn balls, and blindfolds (9 each)

Procedure

Every student is given a task sheet and a pencil. Each student must find someone who can complete one of the tasks stated on the bingo sheet—for example, jump rope 30 times. When classmates perform the task, their name gets written in that space.

Only one name is necessary per space, and no one can sign the same person's sheet twice (unless the class is too small). The first person completely finished must immediately take it to the teacher to be approved and checked for completion. Encourage everyone else to continue until everyone has finished. If time permits, ask questions to see what students learned about others in the class, especially the interesting and odd statements. Prizes to the top finishers are optional. Duplicate copies of the Who's Who card can be made and then cut in half to use in class.

Wide World of Sports

What would physical education be without playing the traditional sports? These fun games incorporate traditional sport skills into vigorous and challenging competitions.

Gotcha Tournament (3-5)

Objective

To provide practice shooting baskets and rebounding both quickly and accurately.

Equipment

- Two different colored basketballs per goal
- Different colored jerseys for teams at each goal

Procedure

Gotcha is a fast-paced basketball shooting game. The Gotcha Tournament works best when implemented after a Basketball Unit. Divide students into even groups based on number of available goals (for example, six goals equal six groups). Each group starts from behind the free-throw line. The first two players in line have basketballs, preferably different colored or different types to avoid confusion.

To begin, the first person in line shoots the ball, followed by a shot by the next person in line. These players continue shooting the ball until someone makes a shot. The only way to be eliminated is if the person behind you makes it before you do. For example, if the first person makes it, the ball immediately goes to the third person in line. The second player should continue shooting, attempting to make a basket before the person behind him or her makes it. If the second person makes it before the first person, the second person goes to the end of the

Jump Rope 30 Times	Shoot 2 Free Throws	Sing Old McDonald Had A Farm	Buddy Walk The Length Of The Gym	Jog 2 Laps Around The Gym
Dribble A Basketball 2 Lengths Of The Gym	Perform Ring Around The Rosie With Someone	Chest Pass A Basketball 10 Times	Hula Hoop Around Your Neck	A Person Who Has 2 Or More Sisters
Yell Something Funny As Loud As You Can	Stork Stand On One Foot For 30 Seconds	Free Space	Birthday Is In December	Perform A Dance
Can Juggle 3 Scarves	Can Do A Layup	Writes Lefthanded	Can Do 10 Pushups	Hop On The Red Line Around The Gym 1 Time
Perform A Cartwheel	Standing Broad Jump At Least 3 Feet	Throw A Ball Into A Goal While Blindfolded	Make Your Goofiest Face	Was Born In Another State

Jump Rope 30 Times	Shoot 2 Free Throws	Sing Old McDonald Had A Farm	Buddy Walk The Length Of The Gym	Jog 2 Laps Around The Gym
Dribble A Basketball 2 Lengths Of The Gym	Perform Ring Around The Rosie With Someone	Chest Pass A Basketball 10 Times	Hula Hoop Around Your Neck	A Person Who Has 2 Or More Sisters
Yell Something Funny As Loud As You Can	Stork Stand On One Foot For 30 Seconds	Free Space	Birthday Is In December	Perform A Dance
Can Juggle 3 Scarves	Can Do A Layup	Writes Lefthanded	Can Do 10 Pushups	Hop On The Red Line Around The Gym 1 Time
Perform A Cartwheel	Standing Broad Jump At Least 3 Feet	Throw A Ball Into A Goal While Blindfolded	Make Your Goofiest Face	Was Born In Another State

line and the first person is out. That person must now go to a designated area (a large, coned-off area), get a ball, and practice dribbling or play one-on-one with a friend. The player shooting always must get the rebound without anyone's assistance. Follow this progression until only one player remains. *Remember, the person who is behind you changes frequently, so don't just remember that the person who started the game is behind you.*

Tournament Format

There are six teams, each designated by different colored jerseys. Send all teams to play at one of six particular goals. When each team is lined up and ready, play begins. After each round, the top two players from each team check in with the teacher and give their names. After the top two players from each team have been established, the teacher stops class. The top two from each team then participate in the playoff round at a central goal to play the top two shooters from the other teams.

All students may gather around and watch during each playoff round to cheer on their representatives, or they may remain at the designated area to continue dribbling or playing one-on-one. There are usually about four to eight playoff rounds, depending on the time. During the last 10 minutes of class, all first place winners from each of the six to eight playoff rounds (at least 10 to 12 finalists) play in one championship round. All other students may gather around or remain at the designated area to continue dribbling or playing one-on-one.

For a fun option, award each champion a trophy to carry around for a week. First, second, and third place finishers can then receive personalized certificates. Old trophies with no specific sport on them are great to use. Students are the ones who know what the trophies represent!

Hockey Mania (3-5)

Objective

To improve participation and sport skills. To maximize success and participate in an aerobic workout. Hockey Mania is an excellent large-class, indoor or outdoor alternative to the traditional floor hockey game.

Equipment

- Soccer or hockey goals (4)
- Hockey pucks or hockey balls (30-75) (depending on if you have a wood or carpeted gym, or if you are playing outside)
- Version A requires enough jerseys to make four even teams. Version B requires four sets of different colored jerseys (6-8 each) to represent each team.
- Version A requires one stick per person. Version B requires 24-32 hockey sticks and is for oversized classes only.
- Sets of goalie gear (4) (only necessary to enhance realism)
- Version B requires traffic cones to section off home bases in each corner of the playing area.

Procedure

Version A is recommended for classes of 25 to 55 children with enough available equipment. Before the class arrives, set out all of the necessary equipment in front of each of the four goals (see Hockey Mania layout *a* on page 107 for setup). On the teacher's signal, instruct students to put on a jersey and get a stick, which are located in front of one of the four goals. Remind students that if there are no more jerseys left in front of a goal, then find a jersey and stick by each of the other goals. Give each team the responsibility of selecting one goalie and two or three defenders for the first round. Everyone else is on offense.

The teacher's signal begins the game. All of the offensive players begin to dribble the hockey pucks (or balls) and attempt to score at any of their opponent's goals. At the same time, all defensive players (remember, only two or three are allowed in front of their team's goalie box) attempt to protect their team's goal. The object of the game is to have the least amount of pucks in your team's goal. Establishing a winner at the end of class is optional. After all the pucks have been scored, immediately stop play and tally the total number of points scored at each goal. It helps if only the goalies are allowed to count pucks to give the teacher their team's total for that round. Upon completion of each round, have students return the pucks to center court, then select new goalies and defenders and begin the next round.

Version B is recommended for exceptionally large classes (55-75) or when not enough equipment is available. First divide the students into four equal teams. Then send each team to the designated corners of the gym, where they can find six to eight jerseys and hockey sticks (see Hockey Mania layout *b* on page 108 for setup). At this time, have each group decide a team name (associated with the team's color). Explain that those who have a stick and jersey are Team 1 for that color, and those who do not have a stick or jersey are Team 2 for that color. Each team decides who is the goalie and who plays defense and offense.

Team 1 from each of the four colors is then called out to the floor. Have students stand outside the center circle, which contain all hockey pucks. Follow the same procedure and rules as in version A. Upon completion of each round, have students return the pucks to center court. Announce Team 2 to come out and trade positions with Team 1. Team 1 now cheers on their color from their designated corner.

Rules and Safety

- ■ Only the goalie may be inside of the goalie box. Place floor tape, Velcro, or chalk on the surface to designate a 10-by-12-foot box.
- ■ Only two or three defensive players may stand outside their team's goalie box to help protect it.
- ■ Absolutely no high sticking! High sticking will result in a penalty box time-out. (Strictly enforce this rule.)
- ■ There are no boundaries in the gym—you can play the pucks off the walls.
- ■ No touching the goalie—shots must be taken from outside the goalie box.
- ■ When a hockey puck goes in and bounces out, it is still a score. All goalies must put all bounced-out shots back in the goal.
- ■ In version B, teams not playing must stay in their designated corners.
- ■ The winning team has the fewest points scored against them.

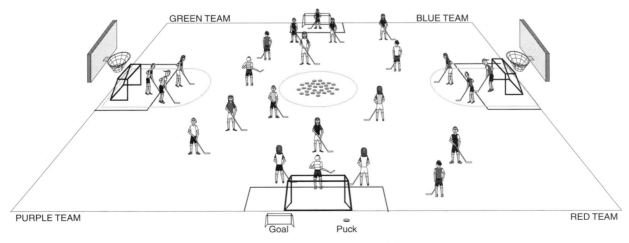

Hockey Mania Layout (a)

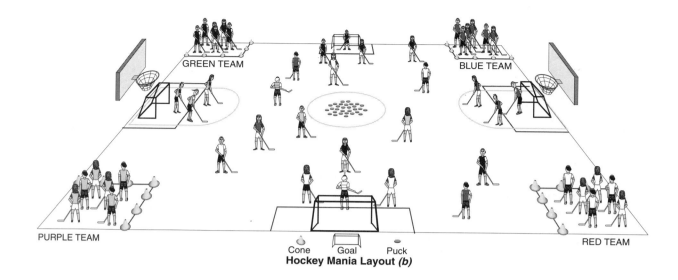

GREEN TEAM

BLUE TEAM

PURPLE TEAM

RED TEAM

Cone   Goal   Puck
Hockey Mania Layout *(b)*

- Start/stop play when you hear the signal.
- Optional: After each game, record the scores. Remember, at the end of the class, the team with the least number of goals scored against them wins!

VARIATIONS

Play Scooter Hockey Mania by adding scooters and using hand-held hockey sticks instead of regular sticks. Hockey stick replacement blades work best (they're cheap and durable, too). Simply follow the same rules as in Hockey Mania. This game also can be tied into your scooter unit. Try this one especially with your P-2 children. They will love it!

Noodle Hockey Mania is an excellent alternative to Hockey Mania as well. Follow version A rules, but replace all hockey sticks with four-foot swim noodles and substitute all pucks with Gatorskin balls. With the P-2 students, just play the game and don't worry about where children must score or how many points each team has. Just get them active and let them play.

Indoor Soccer (P-5)

Objective

To develop kicking, trapping, dribbling, and passing skills in the game-type situation of indoor soccer.

Equipment

- Soccer or hockey goals (2) (As an alternative, tape a four-by-seven-foot box on the wall at each end the gym
- Nerf soccer balls (3 or 4)
- Different colored jerseys to represent each team (2 sets)

Procedure

Divide the class into two equal teams and send them to opposite sides of the gym to put on the colored jersey for their team. The object of the game is to dribble, pass, shoot, and score one of four balls into your opponent's goal.

To begin, place three or four soccer balls into the center circle of the gym. The extra balls keep the groups separated instead of crowding around one ball. On the signal "go," students start handling the balls (feet only), attempting to kick them into their opponent's goal. When the first ball has successfully been scored, stop play immediately to record the score for the scoring team, and have all children bring the balls back to the center circle and start a new round. The team to score the most points wins!

Rules and Safety

- Hands may not touch balls unless it is done to protect the face.
- No one may enter the goalie box. (Place a Velcro box on the floor to protect the goalie.)
- The goalies are the only players who can use their hands legally.
- There are no boundaries; the ball can be played off all of the walls.
- Each team may have no more than three defenders standing outside the goalie box to help block balls.
- The teacher may award penalty shots or points for the violation of any rules as deemed appropriate.

 VARIATION

Turn goals so that they face the walls. Students must then kick the ball off the wall to score.

In the Zone (3-5)

Objective

To learn teamwork and good sporting behavior. To improve passing and catching skills.

Equipment

- Nerf or foam footballs (10-15)
- Traffic cones (to represent end zones) (20)
- Two sets of different colored jerseys (to represent the quarterbacks) (5 or 6 each)

Procedure

In the Zone is a teamwork game where children improve their passing and catching skills while trying to get all their teammates out of their own end zone. Place traffic cones five yards from the end wall, one side of the gym to the other. This represents the end zone (see In the Zone layout on page 110 for setup). Separate the class into two teams, and send each team to their end zone on each side of the gym. Select five or six quarterbacks from each team, have them put on red or blue jerseys, and direct them to stand on centerline of gym.

Explain that on the teacher's signal, the quarterbacks can begin passing the football to their teammates. To leave the end zone, all teammates standing inside their own end zone must catch a ball thrown by their team's quarterback. Once a teammate catches a ball in the air, they immediately must make one of two choices: one, keep the ball and become a quarterback to help pass balls to their teammates to get them out of the end zone, or two, become a defender by going in front of the opposing team's end zone to try to deflect or intercept any footballs. If a defender intercepts a ball from the opposing team's quarterback, the quarterback who threw it must go into their color end zone.

A winner is declared in one of three scenarios. First, when all the players from one team are out of their end zone, that team wins. Second, whichever team has the most players out of their end zone after a predetermined time limit wins. Or, third, if all five or six original quarterbacks are in their end zone as a result of their passes being intercepted, the other team wins.

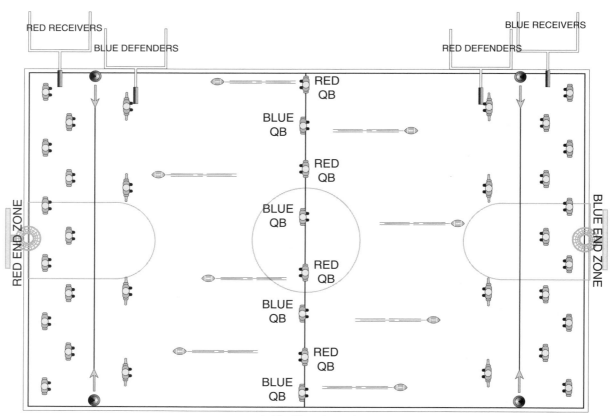

In The Zone Layout

Rules and Safety

■ All quarterbacks must stand on the center line to pass footballs.

■ Footballs must be caught in the air in the end zone. Balls that are deflected and then caught or caught off the walls do count.

■ Defenders cannot go into the opposing team's end zone.

■ If a defender intercepts a ball, the quarterback who threw it must go to their team's end zone.

■ Balls picked up off the ground must be carried to the quarterbacks, or quarterbacks can retrieve the footballs, return to the centerline, and begin passing again.

■ Once out of the end zone, a player must choose to be a defender or quarterback and stay at that position. They may choose differently if they go back to their end zone and get out again.

VARIATIONS

Use indoor foam Frisbees instead of footballs to work on Frisbee throwing skills or use both footballs and Frisbees in the game.

Scoot 'n' Shoot (3–5)

Objective

Each child engages in dribbling, shooting, passing, scooter skills, and strategy in the fast-action teamwork game of Scoot 'n' Shoot.

Equipment

- Trashcans (55-gallon) without wheels (2)
- Five-gallon buckets (4) (2 full of yarn balls and 2 empty)
- Basketballs (10-12) (5-6 one color, 5-6 another color)
- Scooter boards (20-40)
- Jerseys to designate both teams (optional)

Procedure

Before the class begins, place one trashcan, yarn ball bucket, and empty bucket on each end of the gym against the wall (see Scoot and Shoot layout for setup). Divide the class into two teams and have them sit opposite the goal they will be shooting at (the 55-gallon trashcan). Select five players from each team to stand against the wall beside their team's goal on the opposite side of the gym. Instruct all other players to get on scooters.

The object of the game is for each team to score as many baskets as possible within the time limit. The team that wins is the one with the most yarn balls (points) or the one that showed the best teamwork. To begin, five or six players from each team start dribbling their team's designated basketballs from their end line while moving on their scooters. Players without basketballs can spread out and wait for a pass from a teammate or play defense.

Rules and Safety

- All players must dribble when moving on a scooter. When players pick up their dribble, they must either pass the ball to an open player or shoot the ball.
- Defenders may block the opposing team's view or knock basketballs away, but they may not retrieve them.
- Players are not allowed to touch or grab opponents.
- Each team can only dribble and shoot their team's designated color balls.
- Players on scooters may not cross the end line to shoot a basketball. All shots must be made from anywhere inside the end lines.
- If a basket is made, the first person standing in line puts one yarn ball into the empty bucket. That person then gets the scooter and basketball from the teammate who scored and carries them to the opposite side to reenter the game from the sideline. The person

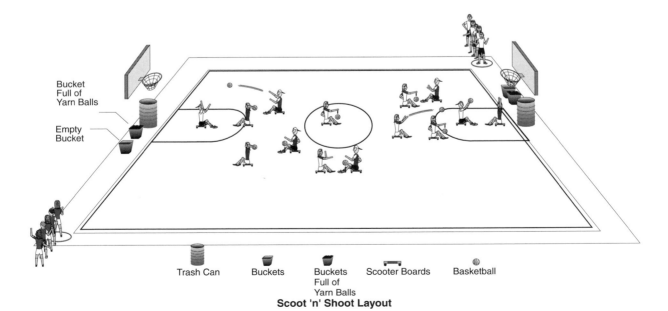

Bucket Full of Yarn Balls

Empty Bucket

Trash Can   Buckets   Buckets Full of Yarn Balls   Scooter Boards   Basketball

Scoot 'n' Shoot Layout

111

who just shot stands at the end of the line. Players typically do not stand for very long because of the quickness of the game and number of balls being used.

- If a defender retrieves an opposing team's ball, they may roll it to the other side of the court.
- A shot that is missed may be rebounded to be shot again.

VARIATIONS

Require each team to pass the ball a certain number of times before taking a shot.

Designate certain shooting lines to represent different points. The game becomes more difficult and results in more yarn balls being dropped in the bucket.

Add more basketballs to increase success, or take some away to increase difficulty.

Scooter Football (3-5)

Objective

Scooter Football is an excellent indoor game that reinforces throwing and catching, agility, cooperation, and cardiovascular fitness.

Equipment

- One scooter per person
- Two different colored jerseys
- One or two Nerf footballs

Procedure

Designate two end zones in the gym, each a different color (see Scooter Football layout for setup), and place enough scooters, based on the number of children, inside each. Divide the class in half, and send each team to the red or blue end zone. Flip a coin to see who gets first possession of the Nerf footballs.

Each team starts at their own end zones. The team who won the coin toss starts the game by throwing the balls to their teammates who are moving down the field. Once players have possession of the ball, they cannot move on the scooter. They must pass the ball forward, backward, or sideways to a teammate. The object of the game is to make enough successful completions to teammates, which eventually lead to a catch in the end zone and result in a touchdown.

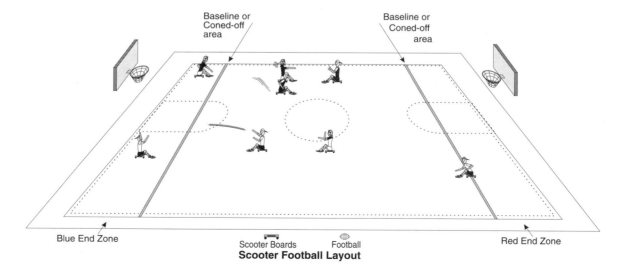

Scooter Football Layout

Rules and Safety

- Defensive players may intercept a pass anywhere and at any time.
- Defensive players may not take a ball from an offensive player unless it is rolling on the ground.
- If a player in possession of the ball falls off the scooter, the other team immediately gets possession of the ball from that point.
- It is a turnover when the ball hits the ground or is dropped or intercepted.
- After a turnover occurs, the recovering team may immediately start play from that point.
- There are no onsides or offsides.
- All players must stay seated on their scooter.
- A player may only stay in the end zone for five seconds.
- The team with the most touchdowns by the end of class wins!

 VARIATION

Add one or two more Nerf footballs to increase the excitement and involvement, especially with larger classes.

 HINTS

Encourage children to make their passes short and easy to catch instead of making long passes. Their success rate will be much greater.

Also, designate student referees to help the teacher notice any rule violations.

Scooter Team Handball (3–5)

Objective

Students engage in passing, scoring, and scooter skills in the fast-paced game of Scooter Team Handball.

Equipment

- Soccer or hockey goals (2) (As an alternative, tape a four-by-seven-foot box on the wall at each end the gym.)
- Scooter (1 per person) (Goalies do not have to be on a scooter.)
- Gatorskin balls, 6-8 inches (3 or 4)
- Different colored jerseys to represent each team (2 sets)
- Lines to represent goalie box (The basketball three-point line works best, or a use the 10-by-12-foot box established from some of the other games.)

Procedure

Designate two goal areas on each side of the gym, placing each goal on the end line under each basketball hoop. Place enough scooters and different colored jerseys, based on the number of children, on each side of the gym. Once the class arrives, divide the class in half, and send each team to either side of the gym to get a scooter, put on a jersey, and wait for more instructions. Flip a coin or have team captains play a game of *Rock, Paper, Scissors* to determine which team gets possession of the balls first.

The team with the balls starts the game by throwing the balls to their teammates who are moving down the court. While players have possession of a ball, they cannot move on their scooter. They must pass the ball to another teammate or shoot at the goal. Play ends once a ball has been scored. Play resumes after both teams have returned to their side and the non-scoring team has possession of the balls.

Rules and Safety

- Once players have possession of the ball, they cannot move on their scooter. They must immediately pass or shoot the ball.
- No one may enter the goalie box. The shot must be taken from outside the clearly marked lines on the floor—a Velcro line or three-point line will be used to represent the goalie box.
- A dropped ball may be picked up by anyone.
- There are no boundaries; the ball can be played off all of the walls.
- Each team may have no more than three defenders outside the goalie circle to help block balls.
- A ball that hits inside the goal (or inside the boundary on the wall) is a score.

VARIATIONS

Allow the goalies to stand.
Play regular Team Handball—no scooters!

Whirlwind Tournament (3-5)

Objective

To implement long-rope jumping skills in combination with the fast-paced, aerobic game of Whirlwind.

Equipment

Long ropes (3)

Procedure

Whirlwind is a fast-paced jumping game. The Whirlwind Tournament works best when implemented after the Jump Rope Unit. At the beginning of class, put girls on one side of the gym, boys on the other. Place one long jump rope on each side of the gym in addition to one rope in the middle for students to practice at once they are out of the regular game. Position children so that no one can run into each other (see Whirlwind Tournament layout for setup). The object of Whirlwind is to be the last person to successfully jump into the rope without getting caught by the rope.

Whirlwind Tournament Layout

Tournament Format

There are six to eight playoff rounds played. The top two winners from each round are documented and earn the right to participate in the championship round at the end of the class. There should be 10 to 12 challengers competing to determine the overall Whirlwind Champion.

To begin, the rope turner starts turning the rope. Once the first person runs in and jumps, the next person has to run in and quickly jump before the rope hits the ground for the first time. This process produces a "whirlwind" effect because someone is always inside the rope jumping with every turn. Again, when the rope passes in front of someone and hits the ground with no one inside that person is out. Every time a successful jump is made, students go to the end of the line to wait the next turn and catch their breath. As children are eliminated, the line gets shorter. The short line eventually causes a circle to form because children are running and jumping rapidly.

This whirlwind effect is quite an awesome sight to see! When the game gets down to two participants, slow the rope turn down to give each person a chance to make it back around.

 HINT

Children can get back in line quicker if they go in at an angle, brushing by one of the rope turners.

 VARIATIONS

Try the Gotcha Tournament format with Whirlwind to see what method works best for you.

Award each champion a trophy to carry around for a week. First, second, and third place finishers can then receive personalized certificates. Old trophies with no specific sport on them are great to use. Students know what the trophies represent!

Part II

Supplemental Ideas for Physical Education

In part I, I describe units and games for educators; in part II, I provide tools to assist educators with other important facets of their jobs. We all know that it is not an easy task maintaining control of large groups of children—especially those who are having fun! In the following chapters, I talk about how you can establish procedures and expectations during the first week of school so that you can more easily corral your students during all of these fun activities.

I also talk about how an understanding can be reached between teacher and students with the use of a valuable technique called the *problem-solving table*. In addition, I describe how you can establish a *payback system* to assist you in helping students learn the consequences of their behavior.

Chapter 3

Ideas for Behavior and Class Management

The first week of school is a time for you to get to know the students while clearly introducing and clarifying class rules, signals, procedures, expectations, and how much fun they are going to have during the year. One of the themes I try to establish early in my own class is accountability. That way, students can develop self-responsibility and learn to use a tool to sort out problems for themselves.

First Week of School

Teachers can establish the tone of the entire semester during the first week of school. The activities in this chapter can help educators get children started with the means to make proper behavior easier to accomplish.

To create an optimum learning environment, teachers should implement a behavior and class management strategy. The following class management procedures can be covered in detail at the beginning of school and then reinforced throughout the year—especially during the first two weeks.

When discussing rules and consequences, make it a point to select, recognize, and praise students who are demonstrating behaviors expected in physical education, such as listening when others are talking and raising their hands to answer questions. This will be a great time to let students know that their teachers and their peers are always observing them. It is important, especially at the beginning of the year, to set the stage for physical education behaviors and expectations. Be sure to provide many examples of behaviors that will be expected from each child. As the school year progresses, frequently "catch" students demonstrating behaviors congruent with class expectations.

Welcome to Physical Education

Ask students to name any activities they would like to do this year and record them for possible future lessons. When you listen to student opinions, it gives them some ownership in what they perform in class.

Establish the Class Signal

Explain that each day follows the same procedure: When the children arrive, the physical education class begins immediately after the teacher gives the signal and everyone is seated, listening attentively. For example, the teacher can say *one-two-three*, and students immediately sit down and respond by yelling *Hoo!* as loud as they can, which is then followed by complete silence. The loud signal (*Hoo!*) gets the attention of all the other students who may not be aware that the teacher is ready to begin class. The teacher gives the signal only

- at the beginning of class to get everyone ready to begin,
- during class when it is time to discuss a new activity or skill,
- to stop the class and reinforce particular rules, or
- to initiate the 10-second countdown.

Get Students Active

After you introduce and practice the class signal, select a game or activity from the games unit to demonstrate and play (see chapter 2, "Supporting Games and Activities"). Remember that class time is limited and that the children are going to be asked to learn a lot of material at the beginning of the year. A strategy that works well is to introduce and play games during the first two weeks of school but save the last part of class for administration. It quickly gets children active at the beginning of class, which makes them more likely to listen during the last 10 to 15 minutes of class when you cover class rules, procedures, and expectations.

Discuss the Classroom Procedures

Determine the class rules based on the facility being used and number of students in attendance. The main points to consider are

- bathroom breaks,
- water fountain usage, and
- entering and exiting the gym.

One example of entering the gym: Show each class which gym line to sit on when they enter and exit the gym. For example, students enter the gym every day and sit on the designated line assigned to them, then they repeat the procedure before they exit the gym. This habit ensures that there is not pandemonium at the beginning and end of class.

Develop a List of Rules and Consequences

For this activity, have the third, fourth, and fifth graders brainstorm new rules and consequences or have them add and delete (at teacher's discretion) to the already established list of rules.

The following is a typical list of rules that you can adapt and display for your students:

- Play and have fun.
- Show respect to others and to the equipment.
- No horseplay or fighting.
- Always play safe.
- No food, candy, gum, or toys in gym.

The following is a list of sample consequences that you can give when a student breaks a rule:

- Verbal warning
- Time-out from the activity
- Trip to the principal's office
- Cleaning tasks while others play
- Note home to parents

 HINT

Briefly review rules and consequences each day during the first two weeks. Point out that students are the ones who helped develop these rules and that they *must* live with the consequences they created.

10-Second Countdown

At the end of class, give students a slow 10-second countdown. During this countdown, students must clean up their area and sit down on their designated line to await the arrival of their teacher. You can also use the 10-second countdown at the beginning of class to quickly group students and instruct them.

Grading Procedures

Because grading procedures, policies, and guidelines vary from program to program, I have listed a few ideas as examples to consider when you determine a child's overall grade in physical education:

■ Participation

■ Behavior

■ Skill proficiency

■ Written test

■ Appropriate dress

Formal and informal assessments and skills tests are not included in this resource. To ensure that you meet your program's objectives and guidelines, you can easily create them by utilizing the skills and concepts presented in this book.

Other Things to Discuss with Third, Fourth, and Fifth Graders

■ "Who's Who in PE?" (play this game the first two days)

■ Fifth grade end-of-the-year Blast-Off!

■ Fifth grade Helpers of the Month

Problem-Solving Table

The problem-solving table is a successful behavior management strategy that places the responsibility of problem solving right in the students' hands. Most of the inappropriate behavior that typically occurs in class is between two students and typically results in a class disruption and a need for intervention by the teacher. This disruption, better known as *tattle telling*, is a frustrating but common problem in many elementary schools. If children become dependent on someone else to solve their problems, then they may never develop responsibility to sort out problems for themselves. In order to reduce recurrences of this problem, try implementing the Problem-Solving Table.

Use a teacher led role-play to achieve understanding of the process and to reinforce the significance of being accountable and handling problems independently. It is best to discuss the problem-solving table during the first week of school. The premise is this. If someone has a problem, instead of telling the teacher, they immediately ask the person involved to go to the Problem-Solving Table. The student then should point to one of the many faces on a poster that best demonstrates how they feel at

Problem Solving Table

121

that moment. The poster depicts a variety of typical emotions that all people experience. Posters of faces can be found in health and wellness catalogs. Students typically point out faces that are sad, angry, frustrated, and hurt. Interestingly enough, many students will begin learning and realizing how their actions sometimes make others feel. Students proceed by discussing their problem and possible ways to solve it by following these steps to solving a problem. List these steps on a poster as a reminder for students.

1. What is the exact problem? Remember to listen.
2. Tell your side of the story; don't play the blame game.
3. Suggest possible solutions and come to an agreement.
4. Carry out your agreement by keeping your word.

Teach students that they can't leave the Problem-Solving Table until both parties have covered all four steps. In some cases both parties can't agree on a solution or resolve their differences. If this occurs, allow students to come to the teacher, not to solve the problem, but to offer suggestions on how to solve it. This idea is an attempt to teach children about self-responsibility. Instruct students that if anyone verbally or physically abuses them, they must immediately inform the physical education teacher.

Over time, the Problem-Solving Table may reveal that the student who does not want to go to the Table is probably the one who caused the problem. If a student refuses to go to the Problem-solving Table, that student must sit out for not attempting to solve the problem.

The Problem-Solving Table, when implemented and reinforced, will do wonders for any physical education program because it provides an opportunity for students to express how they feel while learning how to resolve differences without the mediation of a teacher.

Rules and Expectations

All physical education rules and expectations must clearly be explained and be consistently applied and reinforced throughout the year, especially during the first few months of school. Post all rules in the gym and refer to them frequently when rules are violated. After students become acquainted with the rules, then introduce and discuss the *paybacks system*.

Paybacks System

Consequences, other than verbal warnings, are given in the form of "Paybacks." Paybacks are given to students after repeated warning of breaking a class rule. If a teacher observes that a student is constantly being an interruption in the physical education class, then it is necessary that the student take some responsibility for his or her actions.

As a consequence, students will "pay" the teacher "back" by sitting out or doing odd jobs. These odd jobs may include cleaning gym baseboards, dusting, cleaning windows and doors, cleaning out or straightening up the equipment room, or any other jobs available in your gym. When given the option, most students would rather work than be sent to the office. No other people are involved, and students respect and appreciate the fact that the problem will stay between the teacher and the student.

This system works well for the student who would rather sit out than play. When they learn that they must work as a result of their poor choices, they typically choose to participate and demonstrate the expected behavior.

The administration appreciates this system as well because the majority of the discipline is handled within the confines of the gym and thus limits office visits. The end result: Students realize and live up to class expectations, and the recurrences of inappropriate behaviors diminish.

Although teachers need to document all behavior problems (see "Paybacks Record Sheet" on page 124), only in extreme or repeated cases do you need to contact administrators or parents. Students also know that for each payback they receive during a grading period, two or three points will be subtracted from their grade for that period.

Recording Paybacks

Record each payback on the record sheet. After a sheet is filled, transfer each payback to a five-by-eight index card with the student's name and teacher's name on it. Each time a student gets a payback, record it on the card.

If a child gets three paybacks during a nine-week grading period, send a letter home to their parents to be read, signed, and promptly returned (see sample letter on page 125). The student also must pay back the teacher by cleaning during a Fun Day or a physical education class. Four paybacks results in a parent phone call; five paybacks result in a parent conference. Start the payback system over with each new grading period.

Paybacks Record Sheet

1. Not listening or following instructions
2. Not controlling conversation
3. Not participating within personal space
4. Not showing respect to others
5. Not showing respect to teachers
6. Eating food, candy, gum, or playing with toys during class
7. Not participating in class
8. Not using equipment properly
9. Hitting/roughing, physical abuse, or bullying
10. Inappropriate language
11. Cheating

Name	Date	Number/offense	Comments	Teacher

 From *No Standing Around in My Gym* by J.D. Hughes, 2003, Champaign, IL: Human Kinetics.

Sample Report to Parent

Just a note to let you know that _____ is having difficulty in the following areas:

_____ Listening and following instructions

_____ Controlling conversation

_____ Participating within personal space

_____ Showing respect to other students

_____ Showing respect to the teachers

_____ Eating food, candy, gum or playing with toys during class time

_____ Participating in physical education activities

_____ Using equipment properly

_____ Hitting and being too rough

_____ Using inappropriate language

_____ Cheating during class activity

Comments

Please speak with _____ concerning these matters. If you have any questions or comments, please call us at ***-***-****, or simply respond below.

Date: _____

Thank you,
Coach

Please sign and return tomorrow.

_____
Parent signature

Chapter 4
Student Incentives and Motivational Ideas

While many children love coming to physical education classes, many enjoy additional incentives and motivation. Most students respond well to the additional work that some of these ideas require, and they make the effort worthwhile.

In-School Running Program

An in-school running program is an excellent way to teach students to establish personal goals. Give them the opportunity to run regularly, and many will embrace the challenge.

Objective

Each student participates in a running enrichment program to (1) improve cardiovascular fitness and aerobic endurance, (2) jog or walk around a track for 12 minutes to reach personal goals, and (3) learn proper jogging and muscle-stretching techniques in preparation to jog or walk.

Equipment

- A track, an open grassy area, or a safe parking lot
- Whistle
- Stopwatch
- Counting sticks (500-750) (Tongue depressors work best.)
- Grade book (for documenting each student's laps)
- Traffic cones (to section off areas, if necessary)

Procedure

The running program is held twice a year, once in the fall and once in the spring. The students run 12 times during each nine-week period with one or two designated running days each the week in the semester. Stretch time, run time, and recording time take approximately half of a 40 to 45 minute class.

At the beginning of each running day, all students do various stretches (deemed appropriate by the teacher) to prevent pulled muscles. After warming up, students line up behind the starting line, and the coach blows the whistle to start the running session. Students have the option of jogging or walking. Students who are walking should remain on the outside of the track to allow room for those students who are jogging on the inside of the track. The running proceeds for 12 minutes, and each coach has a stopwatch to inform the students of how much time is remaining to run. After completing a lap, the student receives a stick.

At the end of 12 minutes, students stop running and walking to report to their designated lines (inside the gym or outside). When the students are quiet and listening, the teacher calls out each student's name to record the number of laps completed. Upon completion of each day's running, select a game from the games unit to play for the remainder of the class (set up the game the day before).

A note about recording laps: Don't record laps for kindergartners; instead, give each kindergartner five miles in the fall and five miles in the spring. At the end-of-the-year running assembly, give each kindergartner a certificate and an opportunity to purchase a 10-mile T-shirt. For grades one through five, record laps throughout their entire stay at the elementary school. In other words, make the laps cumulative from year to year. For example, children who start the program in first grade have each year's lap totals added together until they leave the school after the fifth grade.

At the end of each program, give students the opportunity to earn certificates, shirts, hats, awards, and trophies. The following chart acknowledges when a student earns a certificate and the opportunity to purchase a T-shirt.

Table 4.1   Running Program Rewards

Laps	Miles	Certificate	Shirt
35	5	X	N/A
70	10	X	X
140	20	X	X
210	30	X	N/A
280	40	X	X
350	50	X	N/A
420	60	X	X
490	70	X	N/A
560	80	X	X
630	90	X	N/A
700	100	X	HAT
770	110	X	N/A
840	120	X	X

After 125 miles, the total mileage is monogrammed on a golf shirt with a "Super Runner" logo or school mascot emblem.

HINT

Determine how many laps around the track will equal one mile. For example, in the program depicted in this table, seven laps equals one mile.

Assemblies

Hold two assemblies per year to honor the students' achievement in the running program, one in early December and one in May. In fact, during the first week of your running program, motivate students by explaining the running assembly and what it involves. As mentioned earlier, present the students with certificates, shirts, awards, and trophies at this time. Give every student a certificate, and make sure that the physical education teachers and principals sign all the certificates and awards presented. Remember that Partners in Education are great sources for providing the funds necessary to purchase certificates.

In addition, give students the opportunity to purchase T-shirts for $10 (once a mile mark has been reached) twice a year, one during the fall and once in the spring. Half of the estimated cost can pay for the T-shirts, and the other half can go to physical education funds. Send an order form home to the students' parents to give them the opportunity to purchase a shirt for their child. Of course, remind everyone that it is not mandatory to purchase a shirt. Ideally, give the shirts out during the assembly; otherwise, have a small, in-class presentation once students are back in their classrooms.

Special Awards

One way to have fun with the running program is to create various awards that students can attain.

■ Top five male and female runners—the top runners from each grade level who have earned the most laps during each session. All runners receive a certificate and a ribbon stating they were in the top five, and they can earn this certificate in both the fall and spring running assemblies.

■ Gold, silver, and bronze medallists—the top runners from each grade level who have earned the most laps for the fall and spring combined (I combine first and second graders and third, fourth, and fifth graders to reduce costs from the medals). The top student receives a gold medal, second place a silver medal, and third place a bronze medal during the spring running assembly.

■ Teamwork trophy—This award is given to one class in each grade level for demonstrating teamwork and cooperation by getting the most average laps per student as a class (add laps and divide by the number of students in the class). Explain that this trophy could not be won by one person, but by the commitment and encouragement of everyone trying their personal best. Partners in Education are great sources for providing the funds necessary to purchase the five trophies. This award can be presented in both the fall and spring running assemblies.

■ Top male and female runner of the year—Surprisingly enough, this one is not always won by a fifth-grade student. This trophy is presented to the top male and female with the most laps during the entire school year. To give the award some prominence, display a plaque in the gym that lists each year's champions, and reveal the winner's name during the assembly. Have the runner's name and the number of laps run during the school year printed on the plaque.

■ 12 laps in 12 minutes award—Because my staff and I allocated 12 minutes of class time to run, we decided to extend an extra challenge to the students that you may find useful in your class. It is called the Ultimate Comet Running Club. For the children who reach 12 laps in 12 minutes, give them special recognition by announcing their names over the intercom and awarding them certificates at each of the assemblies. Also, to recognize this achievement more formally, display in the gym a plaque that contains each Ultimate Comet Runner's name.

Sample Letter for Running Assembly

Dear Parents:

As you may know, we have just completed the fall session of our running program. All of our students earned a T-shirt (designated by 10, 20, 40, 60, or 80 miles) or a 100-mile hat and a running certificate. In honor of your child's achievement, we would like to invite you, the parents, to attend our running assembly on Wednesday, December 13. Awards and recognition will be given at the following times for each grade level:

Third, fourth, and fifth grade   8:30 - 9:45

Pre-kindergarten and kindergarten   10:00 - 10:50

First and second grade   12:55 - 2:00

We will be presenting the **"Top Five" certificates** for each grade and gender, the **Ultimate Comet Runners,** and awards to the **best running classes** for each grade level during the fall semester.

Also, if you choose to purchase an award for your child, please remember that all shirts and hats purchased will be given out during or after the assembly. We look forward to seeing you there.

Thank you for your support!

Coach

 From *No Standing Around in My Gym* by J.D. Hughes, 2003, Champaign, IL: Human Kinetics.

Sample Running Assembly Program

I. Welcome parents, teachers, and students; physical education teacher introduction.

II. Explanation of running program.

    A. Conducted two times a year, fall and spring.

    B. 12 days of total running over an 8- to 9-week period.

    C. Each run lasts 12 minutes, and during that run each child will collect one stick for each lap produced.

    D. All laps are cumulative from fall to spring, from year to year (give example).

III. The importance of our running program.

    A. Obviously, it emphasizes cardiovascular endurance.

    B. Most important, we feel it improves self-image by creating individual challenges that 9 out of 10 times are achieved with results they can readily see. Poster demonstration: Each lap (starting at the fourth) has been given a certain level name with 12 being the Ultimate Comet Runner.

    C. Parents and Teachers can also take part in the running/exercise program. (How?)

    D. Finally, T-shirt money allows us to purchase the newest and the latest equipment on the market. Parents, please feel free to browse our equipment room.

IV. Presentation of certificates by class.

    A. Read what the certificate says.

    B. Teachers please notify us of misspelled names or if we forget anyone.

    C. Also, teachers please take up certificates after your students have received them.

V. Top five fall runners certificate recognition; read certificate and explain.

VI. Show 100-mile hat and T-shirts for 10, 20, 40, 60, and 80 miles.

VII. Before we get to the medals and teamwork trophies, we would like to thank the following for their contributions and support.

    A. Principals, parents, and students

    B. Printing company

    C. Partner in Education (provided certificates)

    D. T-shirt company

VIII. Upcoming events in spring.

    A. Top three (gold, silver, and bronze) medallists for the year in first, second, third, fourth, and fifth grades.

    B. Top boy/girl runner at school (plaque)

IX. Explain how to become an Ultimate Comet Runner (12 laps in 12 minutes) or a Superior Comet Runner (13 laps in 12 minutes). Show plaques and recognize those who have achieved these honors.

X. Teamwork trophy explanation (why it is called the teamwork trophy). Announce class winners.

XI. Closing remarks to challenge students to establish and obtain new goals for the next running session.

As an incentive for staff and parent participation in fitness improvement, place a record tally sheet in the office during the fall and spring so that they can record their personal minutes of exercise (of their choice). Give your fellow teachers the opportunity to earn T-shirts, which you can present at the running assembly. Students love to see their teachers awarded with T-shirts—plus, it encourages and supports fitness for everyone.

Grading

Establish a certain number of laps that each grade level has to run during each 12-minute run period. Base the lap total using your professional judgment and any past experiences. Require that each child get at least the minimum number established, but make sure that you encourage them to go for more or to establish new goals for themselves. For each half-lap under the required laps, deduct one point from the overall physical education grade (which is 100). Because the first day of running is usually the toughest, skip this procedure the first day and use it the following 11 running days.

Safety Concerns

- Teach students to stretch so that they prevent pulled muscles.
- Designate certain lanes for runners and walkers to prevent any collisions.
- Encourage students to wear appropriate shoes and have them tied so as not to trip.
- Instruct students feeling pain or shortness of breath to walk or sit down.
- Set up cones, if necessary, to block any incoming traffic.

After-School Running Program

Roadrunners originated in 1993 by Kelly Williams, a physical education teacher at Lithia Springs Elementary in Douglasville, Georgia. Since then, Roadrunners has been incorporated into nine schools in Douglas County, making this after-school program one of the largest running groups in the state of Georgia. The purpose for Roadrunners is to not only promote physical activity and healthy lifestyles, but also to provide an after-school running enrichment program for children that offers the opportunity to improve running knowledge and skills, to participate in running events, and to meet other students in the school and the community. The program is also designed to be a self-esteem builder, giving children a feeling of success when they finish a race and challenging them to improve their personal run times for future events.

Roadrunning Program

The following program is the one used at Bright Star Elementary School in Georgia. Remember to send this sort of information to parents to keep them informed.

Roadrunners

Roadrunners Letter to Parents

Dear Parents,

The Roadrunners program is for anyone in kindergarten and grades one through five, and their parents. Practices are held regularly after school from 2:45 to 4:00 P.M. (rain or shine). If it rains, we conduct activities in the gym; otherwise, weather permitting, we run on school grounds. When Roadrunners report to the gym, they check-in, stretch, run, then cool-down with a water or sport drink. Some practices may have guest speakers, or they may be lead by local high school runners. Practice ends no later than 4:00 P.M. Please make arrangements to promptly have your child picked up. If your child is riding home with someone else, please write the physical education department a note or leave a phone message stating whom your child is riding with after practice.

Children must attend all practices unless excused by a note. This running team is conducted and coached like any other after-school extracurricular activity. Only three unexcused absences are allowed for the entire season. (A season is approximately August to November and February to May.) It is important that parents and students remember that the running enrichment program is a privilege and an honor, so children must maintain both academic and behavioral responsibilities in the classroom. We do check report cards, but parents need to help us be aware of any academic or behavioral problems your child may be having in the classroom.

We post races throughout the school year, and we always send information home with your child three to four weeks before the event. Cost for all races is approximately $10 to $15, which includes entry registration and a T-shirt. We encourage both parents and students to run as many races as possible although we require that all runners participate in a minimum of three races to receive a letter (like the ones on a high school letterman's jacket). At the end of the year, we will present the letters to the students at the Roadrunner banquet. Parents need to provide transportation to and from the races.

The following events are tentatively scheduled for this year's Roadrunners.

Clinton Farms Practice and Pizza*	October 19
Halloween Moonlight Race	October 20
Cops Fun Run*	October 28
Burnett Elementary School	November 18
Chapel Hill Biathlon	December 9
Sweetwater Elementary School*	March 3

(continued)

(continued)

Lithia Springs Elementary	TBA
Arbor Station Elementary	March 24
Holly Springs	May 5
Peachtree Jr. Race	June 2

*=These races raise funds for our physical education program.

We will be practicing with other Roadrunners throughout the county at Clinton Farms (a mutual meeting ground) once or twice during the season. At these practices, if available, special guest speakers and cross-country or track stars from local schools are present and usually work out with the children. The practices are in the evening and are followed up by a pizza or hot supper and a time to socialize with other schools. *Parents are responsible for their children at Clinton Farms practices.* Children are *not* required to attend these practices.

In Roadrunners, the safety of your child is the most important priority, especially when we attend race events. One way to easily keep track of your runner at events is with our Roadrunner T-shirt ($7), which is a bright florescent color with the team name on the front. It makes spotting your child much easier during the event. We also prefer that the runners wear black gym shorts for uniformity. The bottom half of the registration form is for T-shirt orders. Please send in order forms ASAP so that we can immediately purchase T-shirts.

To participate, potential Roadrunners need to pay a minimal membership fee of $8. This fee covers the following:

- Sport drink following each practice
- Purchase of Roadrunner letters and bars (a bar represents one Roadrunner season)
- Any necessary Roadrunner equipment

We look forward to having your child as a Roadrunner, and we hope that together we can make this program a fun and successful experience for everyone.

Thanks for you support!
Coach

Registration

It is important that all participants register for a Roadrunning program. Develop a registration form similar to the sample one shown on page 136.

Parent Meeting

Start the program by having a meeting with the parents of interested children. At this time, explain the program and outline the expectations. A sample letter of invitation is provided on page 137.

Roadrunner Captains

Appointing Roadrunner captains, ones who are reliable and likely to complete the program makes your job easier. The captain designation is also an excellent way to bolster a child's self-esteem. A sample assignment document is found on page 138.

Absence Warning

When a child does not show up for the Roadrunner program, the teacher needs to get in touch with the parents. Establish rules for participation and stick to them. A sample absence warning is shown on page 139.

Student Teachers

Here is a fun incentive to use with fourth and fifth graders who excel and demonstrate great attitudes in physical education. This program utilizes fourth and fifth graders as student teachers at various physical education stations for kindergarten through second grade.

Classes may typically consist of 60 to 75 children, so one-on-one feedback and observation is sometimes simply impossible. One plan to help meet each child's needs—while also providing an incentive for the older students—is to solicit the help of fourth and fifth graders. Every two to three weeks, briefly meet with the fourth and fifth grade teachers to get permission to select up to 12 students. The students then help teach a station-format activity to one 40-minute physical education kindergarten, first, or second grade class. Select these students solely on how well they participate and demonstrate appropriate behavior in both physical education and in their classrooms.

On the day they are to teach, the student teachers should arrive five minutes before the scheduled class is to begin. Upon their arrival, briefly meet with them and explain that their jobs as teachers are to clearly demonstrate skills, divide students into groups, monitor behavior, and rotate each group of children. Next, briefly explain each activity station and what the children should learn. From one of the 8 to 10 stations, have them then select the station that they feel most comfortable teaching (although some stations require two people).

As each class arrives, stand at the door and count off six to eight students to send to each station. Have each group sit and listen to the student teachers for instructions and demonstrations. For three to four minutes, each group performs the skills at each station until you give the signal "get ready to rotate." When the signal is given, children need to clean their area for the next group.

On the rotate signal, direct each group to the next station. Student teachers then get ready for the next group to start the process once again.

Roadrunners Registration Form

Child participating (name and grade):

Parent's name: Teacher's name:

Address: Home phone:

                                                  Work phone:

Any illness we need to be aware of: _____

Any medications taken on a regular basis: _____

Name of doctor:

Phone number:

Hospital preference:

In the event of an emergency, I give permission for the person in charge to initiate transportation for my child to the appropriate medical facility.

_____
Parent signature

- -

Please detach and return bottom portion ASAP.

T-Shirt Order Form

Student's name: Grade:

Homeroom teacher's name:

Youth Large _____   Adult Medium _____   Adult XL _____

Adult Small _____   Adult Large _____   Adult XXL _____

Remember: The yearly membership fee is **$8.00**. The cost of the T-shirt is an additional **$7.00** unless you use last year's T-shirt. **All checks must be payable to the elementary P.T.A.**

All monies received are non-refundable.

If paying by check, please write the amount and the check number: $_____ #_____

If paying cash, please write the amount and initial: $_____

 From *No Standing Around in My Gym* by J.D. Hughes, 2003, Champaign, IL: Human Kinetics.

Invitation to Parents

Dear Parents:

Your child has expressed an interest in joining the 2003-2004 Roadrunners. This program is an enrichment program of elementary physical education. Roadrunners have been in existence since 1993 and have grown to be one of the largest running groups in the state of Georgia. Roadrunners are students who want to improve their running knowledge and ability by training one or two days a week to participate in running events around the community. This program offers a wide variety of experiences, from cookouts for the entire family to structured workouts with athletes, coaches, and trainers. If you or your child is interested in learning more about the Roadrunner program and costs, please attend the mandatory parent meeting on **August 28th, 2003 at 6:30 p.m.** in the elementary school cafeteria.

Sincerely,

Coach   Physical Education Specialists

- -
Detach and return bottom portion ASAP.

Parent's signature: Home phone:

Child's name:

Work phone:

Homeroom teacher: Grade:

Roadrunner Captains

You, _____, have been selected as a Roadrunner Captain because of your leadership potential, work habits, character, and behavior. If any qualities are exhibited that are not consistent with the following job descriptions, you will be relieved of your duties. This behavior is expected and should not be asked of you. Remember, this is your team!

Job Description

- Sign in the students, if you are one of the sign-in people.
- Sit at the head of the line in the roll-call squad that you have been assigned to.
- Learn all the names of the students in your squad.
- Report any absences to the coaches when roll is taken.
- Refrain from talking while an adult is talking.
- Lead your group in exercises (they will be expected to do their best).
- Report any behavior to us that is not consistent with what is expected of a Roadrunner.
- Motivate and encourage (don't boss!) your squad to do their best, and you will encourage characteristics from the character education program.

Each Captain is assigned one of the following duties that must be done for each practice:

1. Cleaning up the gym or outside
2. Putting any equipment away
3. Getting sport-drink cooler
4. Cleaning sport-drink cooler

5. Taking any clothes lying around to lost and found
6. Monitoring behavior until parents arrive
7. Handing out upcoming race event or general information

- -
Detach and return bottom portion ASAP

By signing this paper, I agree to do my very best as a Roadrunner Captain. I will set a good example by demonstrating a good attitude, both in and out of school, for my friends and the younger Roadrunners. I will complete all schoolwork assignments and try my very best. I also understand that if I fail to do any of the above things, I will not be allowed to be a Roadrunner Captain.

_____   _____
Your Signature   Parent's Signature

Teacher: _____

 From *No Standing Around in My Gym* by J.D. Hughes, 2003, Champaign, IL: Human Kinetics.

Absence Warning

Teacher: _____

Attention, Roadrunner Parent:

Your child, _____, has (1) not only received a warning for two dismissals but has now accumulated three or more absences since joining the Roadrunners this season, (2) on numerous occasions, failed to complete class assignments, thus dropping grades, or (3) continually demonstrated behavior intolerable for this after-school enrichment program.

As you know from the permission form from the registration packet, any of the problems listed here results in dismissal from the team. In regard to statement 1, a chart posted in the gym shows all practices and race events that we have had this season. Each day your child is present, that day is marked with an "X." The child is marked "A" for being absent or "E" for having an excused absence. According to our records, your child has three or more unexcused absences. If the absence was excused, we were not notified by letter to excuse this absence. If your child has one more unexcused absence, it will result in dismissal from the team, whether it is due to unforeseen circumstances of your own that now do not enable your child to participate, or due to the lack of interest from your child. For matters regarding statements 2 and 3, this letter is to inform you that if the problem persists, we will have no choice but to dismiss the runner from the team. Thank you for your cooperation, and if you have any questions, feel free to contact Coach.

Sincerely,

Coach

I strongly recommend that you try this mentoring model at your school. Younger students really enjoy the extra attention the older students can provide, and the student teachers get to experience firsthand what regular teachers sometimes deal with—both the good and the bad.

Helpers of the Month

Here is a fun incentive to use with third, fourth, and fifth graders who excel and demonstrate great attitudes in physical education. Helpers of the Month assist educators in promoting behavior expectations to other children. This incentive utilizes third, fourth, and fifth graders as physical education helpers in daily setup, cleanup, errands, and other classroom management needs

At the beginning of each year, inform third, fourth, and fifth grade students about Helpers of the Month and the characteristics the physical education teachers look for when selecting these chosen few. These students are selected solely on how well they participate in class and demonstrate appropriate behavior in both physical education and in their classrooms.

At the beginning of each month, the physical education teachers meet and decide on 6 to 10 students (or however many are needed) who demonstrate the kinds of attitudes being promoted in school. For example, if you are picking from the fifth grade, choose one or two students from each class (try to choose new students each month). Once the Helpers of the Month are chosen, their names, teachers, and their times to report for their responsibilities are printed out on two sheets. Responsibilities usually occur before school and in the afternoon. The master copy is posted in the gym, and the other copy is given to the administrators to be announced over the intercom and printed in the upcoming school newsletter. The students selected really get excited about this!

The Helpers of the Month is a great idea because it works two-fold: One, it encourages others—especially those who display appropriate behavior all the time—that good attitudes and behavior do get noticed and pay off. Two, it also provides wonderful, willing helpers to assist in the daily chores that frequently take a great deal of time; thus, it frees up the educator's schedule to prepare for the day's lesson.

I strongly encourage that you implement this idea or something similar in your program. Helpers of the Month make a significant difference at elementary school level. It not only benefits you and your program, but the self-esteem of those involved.

Talent Show

Star Search is an old-fashioned talent show that allows students to show off their talents. It is fun for both children and parents alike. A sample letter to parents describing the program is on page 141. The sample letter can be photocopied for use in your class. It can also be modified to fit your needs or include your school's rules and policies.

Fifth Grade Blast-Off Party

A Blast-Off party is another way to provide an extra incentive for fifth graders. The extra incentive of having a fifth grade, end-of-the-year Blast-Off party was thought of one year when we, the physical education teachers, started noticing an "attitude change" each year, occurring just after the Christmas holidays. After receiving permission from our principal, we began pumping the students up about this exciting party to be held in their honor at end of the year. We frequently informed all fifth graders at the beginning of class that only fifth grade teachers and coaches would be there as chaperons (although we do choose a few select parents to help serve food and drinks). We included fun games and prizes, favorite activities from the year, and great entertainment; we even did a little research and found reasonable rates for DJs and karaoke machines. If they were not reasonable, we would then come up with an agenda of our own.

Star Search Flyer

Dear Parents:

By popular demand, the physical education department will be hosting a talent show on _____ in the gym. We know there are a lot of shining stars within these school walls, ready and willing to show us their talent. Although this event will not be judged, all participants will receive some form of recognition for their efforts. Here are guidelines that must be followed:

- **All** acts and music must be appropriate for school and approved by the coaches. Any act deemed inappropriate will be stopped immediately!
- Acts may be individual or group.
- Practice must be done at home or during recess.
- Costumes, equipment, or props are recommended but not required.
- All acts have a five-minute time limit.

Some Ideas for Acts

Singing, dancing, playing an instrument, doing gymnastics, cheering, doing magic tricks, performing an athletic demonstration, performing comedy or drama skits, or doing any special talent your child may have.

For your child to participate in Star Search 2003, fill out the form below and return to Coach by **no later than** _____.

Schedule for performances are as follows:

- Kindergarten and first grade   8:15 to 9:30
- Second and third grades   9:40 to 11:00
- Fourth and fifth grades   1:10 to 2:20

Parents, please bring your cameras and join us!!!

- -
Please detach and return bottom portion ASAP

My child, _____, has my permission to participate in the Star Search

2003 on _____. My child's talent will be as follows (please be very specific):

_____

If your child is performing as part of a group, please include all members of the act:

_____   _____

_____   _____

_____   _____
Parent's signature   Child's teacher

Fifth Grade Blast-Off

Dear Parents:

Your child is cordially invited to attend an after-school, going-away party put together by the physical education department, PTA, and STAR 94 music. So enjoy a relaxing evening while we exhaust your child one last time! Pizza, snacks, drinks, prizes, and entertainment will be provided along with a number of exciting activities your child has enjoyed throughout the year.

Date: Friday,

Time: From 5:30 p.m. until 8:30 p.m. (Please pick up your child promptly at 8:30.)

Where: Elementary Gym

Cost: $10.00 per child. (This will take care of all the arrangements.)

Make checks payable to *Elementary PTA*.

                                           Thank you! We hope to see your child there!!!!!

                                                                                              Coach

- -
Please detach this portion and return to the gym ASAP

Child's Name: _____ Teacher: _____

I assume all risks of my child's and my participation in this event and I hereby waive, release, and discharge Elementary School and its agents, representatives, and employees from any claims that may arise from my child's or my participation in this event.

Parent's Signature:_____ Telephone Number: _____

 From *No Standing Around in My Gym* by J.D. Hughes, 2003, Champaign, IL: Human Kinetics.

Once we had them pumped up, we began setting the standards that had to be met before anyone would be invited. We decided on a "Three strikes, you're out" policy. In the past, if we had repeated problems during a physical education class, it was generally due to poor class effort or poor class behavior. So we decided that we would give classes their first and second strikes as a whole group. This always got everyone's attention. They thought this was not fair, but to save us lots of documentation, we knew it would be easier to keep up with only those getting their third strike. Now, to be invited to the fifth grade Blast-Off party, each student had to demonstrate and carry out the following guidelines, or they (as individuals) would receive their third strike:

- Always abide by gym rules, especially listening when the teachers are talking.
- Maintain a B-average in school.
- Receive no more than one office visit for poor behavior.
- Always participate and do your very best in physical education.

We also informed students that their classroom teachers could deliver a third strike at any time based on the failure by any student to adhere to these guidelines. Once a third strike was given, the student's name was added to the "not invited to the fifth grade party list," which would be shown at the end of the year to the principal and classroom teachers for their acknowledgment. Students, after a meeting with a physical education teacher, could earn a strike back, but only by demonstrating excellent behavior and maintaining good grades throughout the entire year.

By the end of the year, overall fifth grade attitudes were awesome. The idea proved to be a success; we had created an atmosphere that we had longed for. The Blast-Off party, minus those few students who didn't make it, truly lived up to its name—it was a blast!

So now, we begin every year informing the new fifth graders of what's to come. What is interesting is that they know from previous years that there is this awesome party at the end of the year and that there are some students who are not invited. (Our idea actually grew a reputation!) Although the party takes a little extra effort to prepare, it is nothing compared to the behavior and class management time saved over the long run. On page 142 is a sample letter to parents about a Blast-Off party. The sample letter can be photocopied and used for your class. Be sure to include all pertinent information such as sponsors, cost, and school policies.

Fun Days

Approximately every two weeks you can hold Fun Days at any elementary level. Fun Days are awarded to each class for demonstrating cooperation and teamwork and for following class rules each week in physical education. Fun Days are great incentives to promote positive behavior and performance during the week, and it is also a day for the teacher to actively participate with the children. It is child's play at its best, with no teacher interference. After having your first Fun Day, your students will want to earn it again and again.

Fun Days provide each child an opportunity to explore and participate in a variety of developmentally appropriate activities to help develop and improve motor performance and social skills.

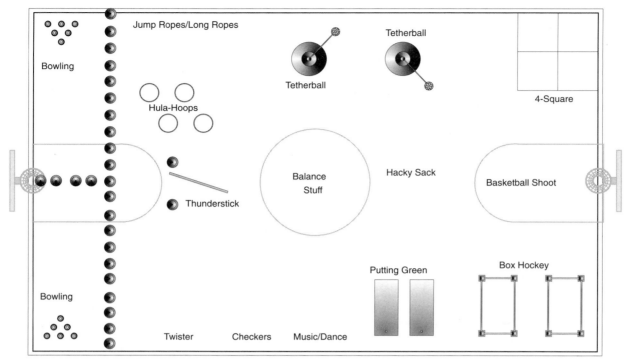

Fun Days Layout

Do a quick demonstration of each activity the first few times you do a Fun Day. Then, as long as all rules are followed, each student may participate at any of the activity stations of their choice, at any time during class. Choose activities from this list or others that you prefer. See Fun Days layout for setup.

Scooters	Box Hockey
Wall Ball	Ping-Pong
Soccer Shoot-Out	Pogo Sticks
Volleyball	Buddy Walkers
Grab the Flag	Zoom Ball
Whirlwind	Skeleton Poly-Parts
Twirl-a-Loops	Balance Master
Wobbler	

Chapter 5

Informing and Educating Parents

Our goal, as a result of a well-designed physical education program, is that children develop healthy attitudes that eventually lead to a lifestyle of regular physical activity. For parents, our goal should be that they understand the important contribution physical education makes towards the quality of each child's life. If we educate the parents, we can help dismiss any negative parental attitudes and have them help promote physical education for years to come.

This chapter not only contains ideas to promote the physical education program, but ideas to inform parents of upcoming events. Parents need to be well informed of what their children learn and do in physical education. From physical education brochures to informative newsletters, it is important that physical educators gain and keep the support of not only parents, but also administrators and colleagues alike. When all of these groups recognize how important physical education is to the overall development of the youth of today, it makes our job as educators much easier to perform.

Brochure

The physical education brochure is an excellent hands-on promotional resource for parents to read that opens and establishes effective lines of communication. The tri-fold, front-and-back brochure is easy to create and makes for an easily accessible resource. Its main purpose is to list and describe objectives and activities, classroom management guidelines, grading policies, and any other relevant information necessary in defining the physical education program in more detail. Teachers can give out brochures at the beginning of the year during open house or send them home with each child the first week of school. Make sure that you keep them during the year so that you can give them to parents anytime a new child is enrolled.

PROMOTE YOUR ACTIVITES

In the following section, I have detailed each step for creating a brochure, for elementary physical education. If you want to enhance and individualize the physical education brochure, you can use great additions such as school colors and mascots. Here are some steps to consider as you develop a physical education brochure.

1. Use a computer program that has brochure capabilities (e.g., Microsoft™ Word, Office, Printshop).

2. Select the material, graphics, scanned pictures, colors, and fonts to include in the brochure.

3. Decide whether to use color or black and white brochures. Black and white copies are cost efficient and easier to reproduce, but color brochures are nicer. I recommend that if you want to produce color copies that you find a local sponsor or Partner in Education to support your program by reproducing color copies.

Newsletter

The physical education newsletter is an excellent hands-on promotional resource that can be sent home to parents to open and establish effective lines of communication. Newsletters are easy to create, and they make for an easily accessible resource. They can be used to list and describe objectives and activities, classroom management guidelines, grading policies, and any other relevant information necessary in defining the physical education program in more detail. Combine the newsletter with the school newspaper, or establish a date each month to send home noteworthy physical education news.

Student Information Card

The physical education student information card is a convenient and easy way to welcome parents and get important health information, phone numbers, and parent volunteers. Sending information cards along with the physical education brochure works best, or you can simply give the cards to each homeroom teacher to send home at the beginning of the school year. Parents need to complete and return cards as soon as possible to the physical education teachers. I recommend storing them alphabetically by grade or by teacher in an index cardholder box. This system provides easy access to parent names, phone numbers, and regular or restricted program information.

Finale

The physical education finale is a video culmination that reflects on physical education learning experiences, activities, and accomplishments during the school year. It provides an opportunity to bring students, teachers, and parents together for one final memorable occasion. I have found that an effective media tool to present a video finale is Microsoft® PowerPoint®.

PHYSICAL EDUCATION
STUDENT INFORMATION CARD

TEACHER _____   GRADE _____

NAME: _____   _____   _____
       Last   First   Middle

STREET ADDRESS: _____

                                          HOME
BIRTHDATE: _____ _____ _____   PHONE: (_____) - _____
           Month   Date   Year

PARENTS OR GUARDIANS: _____

Mother's Employer: _____   PHONE: (_____) - _____

Father's Employer: _____   PHONE: (_____) - _____

Please indicate here with an X if you can volunteer in the Physical Education program in any of the following areas:
Running Errands ☐, Road Runner Helper (after school) ☐, Making Phone Calls ☐, Doing Letters on the Computer ☐,
Fund Raiser Committee ☐.

Important information on Back of Card (Please Fill Out)

To ensure success, make sure you include in the video photographs from the following list:

- Action shots in physical education
- Popular lessons
- Extracurricular activities
- Field days
- Assemblies
- Awards and recognition
- Funny occasions
- Inspirational or sentimental moments

Teachers can also use the video for educational purposes.

- They can show the younger children some of the things they can look forward to in physical education in years to come.
- They can use it as an excellent way to promote their programs, especially when they show it during open house at the beginning of the year.
- They can use it as a fundraiser—when parents see the video and footage of their own children, they may just want to purchase a copy for themselves.

Suggested Readings and References

Cavert, C., and S. Sikes. 1997. *50 ways to use your noodle*. Tulsa: Learning Unlimited Corporation.

DeMarco, T., and K. Sidney. 1990. Enhancing children's participation in physical activity. *Journal of School Health*. 55(6):58-62.

Graham, G., S.A. Holt-Hale, and M. Parker. 1993. *Children moving: A reflective approach to teaching physical education*. 3d ed. Mountain View, CA: Mayfield.

Hinson, C. 1995. *Fitness for children*. Champaign, IL: Human Kinetics.

Landy, J., and M. Landy. 1992. *Ready-to-use P.E. activities for grades K-2*. New York: Parker.

Landy, J., and M. Landy. 1992. *Ready-to-use P.E. activities for grades 3-4*. New York: Parker.

Orlick, T. 1978. *The cooperative sports and games book*. New York: Pantheon Books.

Orlick, T. 1982. *The cooperative sports and games book*. 2d ed. New York: Pantheon Books.

Ratlife, T., C. Imwold, and C. Conkell. 1992. What do your kids really think about their physical education classes?: Procedures teachers use to find out. *Florida Alliance for Health, Physical Education, Recreation and Dance*. 35:32-35.

Schutz, R.W., F.L. Smoll, F.A. Carre, and R.E. Mosher. 1985. Inventories and norms for children's attitudes toward physical activity. *Research Quarterly* 56(3):256-265.

Tinning R., and L. Fitzclarance. 1992. Postmodern youth culture and the crisis in Australian secondary school physical education. *Quest* 42:287-303.

Thomson, J. 1998. *Making a difference in physical education*. Louisville, KY: UNEEDPE.

Thompson, M. 1993. *Jump for joy!* New York: Parker.

U.S. Department of Health and Human Services. 1996. *Physical Activity and Health. A Report of the Surgeon General*. Atlanta, GA: Centers for Disease Control and Prevention.

About the Author

Courtesy of Ronnie Wolf Photography

J.D. Hughes, EdS, is an award-winning educator who has been teaching elementary physical education since 1995. He has published educational games and ideas in *Great Activities,* a newspaper for elementary and middle school physical education teachers. Hughes earned his master's of education in HPED from the State University of West Georgia in 1997, specialist in education in 1999, and National Board for Professsional Teaching Standards certification in 2001. He lives with his wife, Beth, and two daughters in Winston, Georgia, and enjoys exercise and weight training, playing men's softball, and coaching high school softball. J.D. invites you to contact him via e-mail at pe2thmax@bellsouth.net. He welcomes any questions or comments you might have about *No Standing Around in My Gym* including purchasing additional copies.